THE HAND OF THE

FATHER

Breaking Free

from the Anchor

of our

Painful Past

Acknowledgments

I would like to convey my special thanks to my wife, Carole, who had faith in her husband and always knew this work would come about.

THE HAND OF THE

FATHER

Breaking Free from the Anchor of our Painful Past.

By

Dr. Gerard A. Ball DCCPsych

First published 2025

Please send all inquiries to:

info@oceanbiblicalcounseling.com

Dr. Gerard A. Ball DCCP

Disclaimer

This review is intended for informational and educational purposes only. This work is not a medical journal, nor does it purport itself to be one. In no event shall its authors, publishers, suppliers or partners be liable for any damages (including without limitation, damages for loss of data or profit, or any other arising out of the use or inability to use the materials in this guide). Readers are advised to conduct their own research and due diligence and consult with qualified professionals before making any decisions.

Table of Contents

INTRODUCTION

For many non-believers and many believers, the idea of seeing the God of the universe as a "Father" might feel unfamiliar or distant. However, for Christians, this relationship should lie at the heart of their faith and shape their understanding of the Devine. While relating to God as Father isn't a new concept, many contemporary Bible students view it primarily as a perception introduced by Jesus in the New Testament. They might cite passages like the Gospel of Matthew's "Our Father" prayer as evidence. This prayer, often quoted across denominations, does demonstrate how Jesus personally related to God, for He was portraying a deep, intimate connection with Him as "Father."

But what if this relationship wasn't something Jesus introduced? What if it was a foundational truth about God, deeply rooted in Scripture and integral to the way humanity has always been designed to relate to Him? This perspective will change how we see texts like Matthew 6: they are not new revelations but restorations that reemphasize the timeless truth about God's role as our Father.

Let's state something clearly…Throughout both the Old and New Testaments, God reveals Himself as a loving, protective, and guiding Father. From the earliest stories in Genesis, we see this paternal care. For instance, in Genesis 6, the phrase "sons of God" which may very well emphasize an intimate relationship between God and humanity. This is not a new idea introduced in later texts, but a principle established from the beginning. The themes of worship, obedience, and God's fatherly discipline all trace back to these origins, which shows us that God as Father has always been central to His revelation to humanity.

When Jesus taught His disciples to pray by addressing God as "Our Father," He wasn't presenting a novel concept. Instead, He was reigniting an understanding of a relationship that had been obscured over time. Similarly, Paul's reference to God as "Abba Father" in his letter to the Romans reinforces this close, loving connection that mankind should have had with his God from the beginning.

The Challenge of a Distorted Image

While this relationship is foundational to Christian theology, not all believers experience it the same way. For some, the word "father" conjures negative emotions; it can be memories of demanding, abusive, or absent earthly fathers.

When someone's primary experience of fatherhood is broken or painful, it can profoundly affect how they relate to God. Instead of seeing the Devine as a loving and present Father, they may struggle with feelings of detachment or even fear, making the idea of God as "Abba Father" difficult if not impossible to embrace.

This disconnect creates a spiritual barrier. This causes some to have a distorted image of fatherhood and find it hard to trust in God's love and care. Even as they hear sermons or read scriptures about God's unconditional love, these messages can feel alien or unattainable. If you are suffering from this, it is important to know that you are not alone. This is a reality for many who are trying to find their way to the Father. As pastors, biblical counselors, and spiritual leaders, it's crucial to recognize how these early, ingrained perceptions can impact someone's faith journey. For those who have been deeply wounded by their earthly fathers or father figures, understanding God as a loving Father may require careful guidance, healing, and restoration. It might not be easy, but this is where the power of a risen holy Savior comes into play.

This book seeks to highlight these challenges and offers a starting point for addressing them. By using secular assessments and spiritual tools, we can better identify the effects of distorted father images and help those in our care to grow in their relationship with God. For those who may be struggling in this area, this book may help you by pointing out "signposts" in the past that have now loomed to block your journey in finding an abiding relationship with the God of the Bible. The goal is not only to bring healing but also to help individuals experience the peace and ministry that flow from knowing the immeasurable love of our Abba Father.

A Path Toward Healing

For believers trapped by these subconscious distortions, the journey to embrace God as Father is transformative. It involves breaking free from the anchor of past pain and stepping into the Reality of God's eternal love. This process requires patience, understanding, and your broader focus on reconnecting with the Father Who has always desired a deep relationship with you. It is only when we have broken out of this pain and distorted understanding that we fully experience the freedom, joy, and purpose found in our identity as children of a loving Father.

To that end this book is dedicated. It is my prayer that by the end you will have re-evaluated that relationship with the God of the universe. Our Father

Dr. Gerry Ball

CHAPTER 1: UNDERSTANDING ATTACHMENT

Why do some people trust easily while others keep their distance? Why do some friends cling too tightly while others seem emotionally distant? The answers often go back to our childhood and something psychologists call "attachment." Attachment is basically how we learned to connect with people when we were babies and toddlers. The relationships we had with our parents or caregivers back then created patterns that we still follow today - in our friendships, dating relationships, at work, and even in how we relate to God.

In this chapter, we'll explore what attachment is, the different types of attachment styles people develop, and how these styles show up in our daily lives. Understanding attachment can help you make sense of your own behavior and the behaviors of the people around you. Whether you're trying to build healthier relationships or trying to understand why certain situations feel difficult, this knowledge gives you tools to grow. As you read, you'll discover that attachment theory helps you understand not just others, but yourself also.

THE STRANGE SITUATION: A FAMOUS PSYCHOLOGY EXPERIMENT

I believe, one of the most important studies about attachment is called "The Strange Situation." It was created by a psychologist named Mary Ainsworth in the 1970s. She wanted to understand the bond between babies and their parents or caregivers.

Before creating this experiment, Ainsworth had studied families in Uganda (1967) and Baltimore (1971, 1978). She watched how parents and babies interacted and noticed that some parents were really good at responding to their baby's needs, while others weren't as attentive. These observations helped her create the Strange Situation experiment.

The experiment was pretty straightforward but revealed a lot. Ainsworth brought in babies (usually between 9 to 30 months old) with their parents and put them through a series of situations. Sometimes the parent would leave the room, sometimes a stranger would come in, and then the parent would come back. Researchers watched carefully to see how the babies reacted.

What made this experiment so important was that Ainsworth proved something that challenged earlier thinking. Before her work, psychologists thought attachment was simple - you either had it or you didn't. But Ainsworth showed that attachment quality varies a lot from person to person. Some babies had strong, healthy attachments while others had weaker or more complicated ones.

WHAT AINSWORTH DISCOVERED: FOUR ATTACHMENT STYLES

By watching how babies reacted during the Strange Situation, Ainsworth and other researchers identified four main attachment styles. Later studies showed that these same styles show up in adults too!

1. Insecure/Avoidant (Group A)

These babies acted like they didn't really care when their parent left or came back. They would:

• Barely look at their parent when they returned

• Turn away or avoid getting close

• Act almost the same with strangers as with their parents

• Show some distress when alone, but researchers thought they were more upset about being by themselves than missing their parent

Basically, these babies had learned not to depend on their caregivers for comfort.

2. Secure (Group B)

These babies had the healthiest attachment style. They would:

• Feel comfortable exploring the room and playing with toys when their parent was there (using the parent as a "home base")

• Clearly prefer their parent over strangers

• Get upset when their parent left

• Seek comfort and closeness when their parent came back (like hugging or wanting to be picked up)

These babies trusted that their parents would be there for them, so they felt safe to explore but also knew they could come back for comfort when needed.

3. Insecure/Ambivalent or Resistant (Group C)

These babies showed confusing, mixed-up behaviors. They would:

• Want to be close to their parent but then push them away (like reaching out but then squirming to get free)

• Seem angry or frustrated with their parent

• Stay close to their parent instead of exploring, often clinging a lot

It was like they wanted comfort but didn't fully trust that they'd get it, so they acted confused and conflicted.

4. Disorganized/Disoriented (Added in 1986)

About ten years after Ainsworth's original study, researchers Mary Main and Erik Solomon found a fourth type. These babies:

• Had no consistent pattern—their behavior seemed all over the place

• Looked confused or even scared of their parent

• Might try to approach their parent but also back away at the same time

This style often showed up in babies who experienced confusing or scary situations with their caregivers.

HOW THE STRANGE SITUATION EXPERIMENT WORKED

The experiment had eight short episodes (each about three minutes long). Here's what happened:

1. Introduction: The parent and baby entered a room with toys

2. Exploration time: The parent sat down while the baby played

3. Stranger arrives: A new person came in, talked to the parent, then approached the baby. The parent left.

4. First separation: The baby stayed with the stranger

5. First reunion: The parent came back and the stranger left. Then the parent left again.

6. Second separation: The baby was completely alone

7. Stranger returns: The stranger came back

8. Second reunion: The parent returned and picked up the baby while the stranger left

The researchers were looking at four main things:

• EXPLORATION: Did the baby feel safe enough to play and explore?

• SEPARATION ANXIETY: How did the baby react when the parent left?

• STRANGER ANXIETY: How did the baby act around the stranger?

• REUNION BEHAVIOR: How did the baby respond when the parent came back?

These reactions revealed a lot about the quality of the parent-child relationship and how well the baby could handle stressful situations.

WHY THIS EXPERIMENT MATTERS

The Strange Situation gave psychologists a clear way to see and measure attachment. It supported John Bowlby's theory that attachment is a natural part of human development that deeply affects both who we are now and who we become later.

Ainsworth's research showed something really important: HOW a parent responds to their child makes a huge difference. When parents are sensitive and responsive—meaning they consistently notice and respond to their child's needs (like picking them up when they cry or comforting them when they're upset)—children tend to form secure attachments.

Securely attached children grow up with several advantages:

• BETTER EMOTIONAL CONTROL: They're better at managing their feelings, even in tough situations

• BETTER SOCIAL SKILLS: They're good at making friends and handling conflicts because they learned to trust others

• MORE RESILIENCE: They bounce back from stress and setbacks more easily

On the flip side, when parents are inconsistent or don't respond well to their children's needs, kids can develop insecure attachment styles. This can lead to problems with emotional control, higher anxiety, and difficulty building strong relationships as they grow up.

LONG-TERM EFFECTS: HOW BABY ATTACHMENT AFFECTS YOUR WHOLE LIFE

The Strange Situation showed us that early attachment doesn't just matter when you're a baby—it follows you into adulthood. Children with secure attachments typically grow into adults who:

• Are emotionally stable

• Have healthy self-esteem

• Build strong, trusting relationships

Children with insecure attachments may face:

• Trust issues

• Problems managing emotions

• Mental health challenges (like anxiety or depression)

Here's something else Ainsworth discovered: attachment patterns can be passed down through generations. Parents who had secure attachments as kids are more likely to raise securely attached children. But parents with unresolved attachment issues might unintentionally create insecure attachments in their own kids—even if they're trying their best. This is why early support for parents is so important—it can help break negative cycles.

REAL-WORLD IMPACT

The Strange Situation didn't just help psychology professors write papers—it actually changed how we help families in the real world:

• PARENTING PROGRAMS: Programs now teach parents how to be more sensitive and responsive to their children's needs

• THERAPY: Therapists often explore people's early attachment experiences to help them understand and fix emotional or relationship problems

• SCHOOLS AND CHILDCARE: Teachers and childcare providers create environments that help children feel secure

• ADOPTION AND FOSTER CARE: The Strange Situation helps assess what children in foster care or adoption need and guides caregivers in building healthy relationships

A "NEW WAY" OF STUDYING RELATIONSHIPS

Before the Strange Situation, attachment theory was mostly just ideas. Ainsworth gave researchers a practical, scientific method to study how children bond with their caregivers. She proved that attachment isn't one-size-fits-all—it varies a lot depending on each child's experiences.

Her work opened the door for new research on how different attachment styles develop and how traumatic experiences (like neglect or abuse) affect attachment, especially with the later discovery of the "disorganized" attachment style.

CULTURAL DIFFERENCES MATTER

While the Strange Situation has been used all over the world, studies have shown that culture affects attachment behaviors. For example:

• JAPANESE BABIES often show more ambivalent behaviors. This makes sense because Japanese culture emphasizes very close mother-child relationships, with mothers expected to be extremely responsive to their babies' needs.

• GERMAN BABIES are more likely to show avoidant behaviors. German culture values independence and self-reliance more, so parents might encourage children to be more self-sufficient and less emotionally dependent.

These cultural differences suggest that what looks like "insecure attachment" in one culture might just be normal behavior in another culture. The Strange Situation was created in Western (American) culture, so it might not perfectly apply everywhere.

INDIVIDUAL DIFFERENCES

Besides culture, other factors affect attachment styles:

• TEMPERAMENT: Some babies are naturally more social and easy-going, while others are more introverted or difficult. Research by Schaffer and Emerson (1964) found that naturally sociable babies are more likely to form secure attachments, while temperamentally difficult babies might struggle more.

• ENVIRONMENT: Consistency matters! Children who grow up with caregivers who are inconsistent or don't respond to their needs often develop insecure attachment styles.

• PARENT-CHILD RELATIONSHIP: A parent's mental health, stress levels, and emotional availability all affect their child's attachment.

Psychologist John Bowlby proposed something called the "transactional model" of attachment. This fancy term just means that attachment is shaped by both the child AND the caregiver— they influence each other. A child's temperament affects how the parent responds, and the parent's responsiveness affects the child's attachment style. It's a two-way street.

LIMITATIONS AND CRITICISMS

Despite being super influential, the Strange Situation has some problems:

• CULTURAL BIAS: It was created in Western culture and might not work the same way in other cultures

• SHORT-TERM SNAPSHOT: It only shows a brief moment in time, not the complete picture of a relationship

• ETHICAL CONCERNS: Deliberately making babies upset by having their parents leave raises questions about whether the experiment is completely ethical.

STILL RELEVANT TODAY

Despite these limitations, the Strange Situation remains one of the most important studies in psychology. It has inspired tons of research and real-world programs aimed at helping children develop secure attachments.

The discovery of disorganized attachment by Mary Main and Erik Hesse expanded attachment research even more, linking early attachment patterns to mental health later in life. Disorganized attachment has been connected to higher risks of psychological problems, which shows why early intervention is so important for at-risk children and families.

CONCLUSION

Mary Ainsworth's Strange Situation is a landmark experiment that gave us incredible insights into how relationships work. By systematically watching how babies respond when their parents leave and come back, Ainsworth proved that how sensitive and responsive a caregiver is makes a huge difference in creating secure attachments.

Even though the Strange Situation has some limitations, it has had a lasting impact on psychology and continues to help us understand human relationships and development. More importantly, it helps us understand ourselves—why we act the way we do in relationships, what we need from others, and how we can build healthier connections moving forward.

CHAPTER 2: HOW EARLY ATTACHMENT AFFECTS FUTURE RELATIONSHIPS

The relationships formed in infancy are more than just emotional bonds; they are the foundation upon which the ability to connect, trust, and interact with others is built. Early attachment experiences shape not only an immediate sense of security and comfort but also long-term relational patterns, influencing how individuals approach trust, intimacy, and conflict in adulthood.

This chapter explores how early caregiving experiences, especially interactions with parental figures, profoundly impact attachment formation, personality development, and even spiritual connections. By understanding these dynamics, one can better appreciate the foundational role of early experiences in fostering healthy connections both personally and spiritually.

JOHN BOWLBY'S THEORY: THE FATHER OF ATTACHMENT RESEARCH

John Bowlby is widely regarded as the founder of attachment theory. He made groundbreaking contributions to understanding how the bond between infants and their caregivers affects emotional and social development throughout life.

One of Bowlby's most important observations was about what happens when babies are separated from their caregivers. He noticed that infants go through three distinct stages when separated from their parents for extended periods: protest, despair, and detachment. These stages illustrate the infant's instinctive attempts to reestablish connection, what happens when those efforts fail, and how they eventually shut down emotionally to protect themselves. These early reactions don't just reflect immediate distress—they actually set patterns for how people handle relationships throughout their entire lives.

THREE PHASES OF SEPARATION

Phase 1: Protest

In the protest phase, infants exhibit intense distress when separated from their caregivers. Observers will see them crying loudly, screaming, reaching out desperately, and trying everything they can to get their parent back. These aren't random reactions—they're survival instincts. Bowlby explained that babies are biologically programmed to do whatever it takes to get their caregiver to return. From an evolutionary perspective, this makes sense: an infant alone in the wild wouldn't survive long, so babies are hardwired to sound the alarm when their protector disappears.

Phase 2: Despair

If the separation continues despite all the infant's protests, the child enters the despair phase. This is heartbreaking to observe.

The baby becomes withdrawn and quiet, shows signs of deep sadness, seems to give up hope, and stops actively trying to get the caregiver back. The crying might stop, but the emotional pain remains very real. The infant begins to internalize the loss, meaning they start to believe that perhaps their caregiver isn't coming back. This can seriously damage their developing sense of security and hope.

Phase 3: Detachment

If the situation continues long enough, infants enter the detachment phase. At this point, they appear emotionally "fine" or indifferent when the caregiver returns. They act as though they no longer care and appear emotionally self-sufficient. Here's the crucial understanding: this indifference is not genuine. Bowlby was clear about this point. The baby hasn't stopped caring - they've simply built an emotional wall to protect themselves from more pain. It's a defense mechanism. Inside, the infant has internalized feelings of loss, mistrust, and abandonment. This emotional shutdown might help them cope in the short term, but it can cause serious problems later in life, especially with forming close relationships.

HOW CAREGIVERS BUILD TRUST (OR DON'T)

Building on Bowlby's work, other researchers such as James and his colleagues studied what makes some babies feel secure while others don't. They found that consistency is the key ingredient.

Consistent caregiving means being predictable, so the infant knows what to expect, responding to the baby's needs quickly and appropriately, providing nurturing and loving interactions, and being emotionally available when the child needs support. When caregivers are consistent in these ways, babies develop what's called a "secure base." This means they feel safe enough to explore the world around them because they know their caregiver will be there if they need help. This sense of security becomes the foundation for healthy relationships later in life.

However, when caregivers are inconsistent—sometimes responsive, sometimes not; sometimes loving, sometimes distant—babies become confused. They can't predict what will happen, so they never feel truly safe. The world seems unreliable, and their caregivers seem unpredictable. This uncertainty creates anxious or avoidant attachment patterns that persist into adulthood.

Adults with anxious attachment often act clingy in relationships, harbor an intense fear of being abandoned, constantly need reassurance that they're loved, worry excessively about their relationships, and feel as though they love more than they're loved in return. Where does this originate? It stems from those early experiences of inconsistent caregiving. As infants, they never felt fully secure that their caregiver would be present, so as adults, they're perpetually worried their partner might leave.

Conversely, adults with avoidant attachment tend to have difficulty trusting others, suppress their emotional needs by pretending they don't need anyone, value independence over closeness, keep people at arm's length emotionally, and feel uncomfortable with too much intimacy. This pattern originates from having caregivers who were emotionally unavailable or dismissive. These individuals learned early on that reaching out for comfort doesn't work, so they stopped trying and convinced themselves they don't need anyone.

BARRIERS TO HEALTHY ATTACHMENT

Researcher Wilson identified that when attachment is insufficient or disrupted in childhood, it creates serious risk factors for emotional and relational problems. When caregivers don't provide consistent emotional availability, sensitivity, or responsiveness, children struggle to form secure bonds.

One of the most common results is what researchers call ambivalent relationships. Children with disrupted attachment often have confusing, contradictory feelings in their relationships. They might want to be close but also feel resentful, cling to people but simultaneously push them away, or desperately desire connection while fearing being hurt. This occurs because they deeply want closeness but don't trust that people will remain present or treat them well. This pattern often continues into adulthood, where individuals oscillate between seeking intimacy and being afraid of vulnerability.

Another consequence involves struggling with negative moods. Without secure attachment, children often struggle with emotional regulation, meaning they have difficulty managing stress and difficult feelings. This can lead to persistent anxiety, chronic sadness, frequent anger, and mood swings. These emotional struggles can become permanent patterns, potentially leading to depression or anxiety disorders that persist into adulthood.

Wilson also emphasized that early attachment problems can predict future psychological challenges. Children who experience disrupted attachments face a higher risk of developing serious conditions such as Reactive Attachment Disorder, or RAD, which makes it extremely difficult to form close relationships and manage emotions effectively.

THE "DIVIDED SELF" THEORY

Psychologist William Kirwin offers a fascinating perspective on what happens inside people who experienced broken early attachments. He calls this phenomenon the "divided self." The divided self is essentially an internal split that occurs when a child's attachment needs aren't met. Instead of developing one unified sense of self, the person develops two conflicting internal parts.

The first part is what Kirwin calls the Needing Self. This is the vulnerable aspect that still needs love, connection, and validation. It longs for the security and the care that was never received as a child and represents the authentic emotional needs all humans possess. This part never stops wanting to be loved and accepted.

The second part is the Rejected Self. This is the protective aspect that is formed from repeated experiences of neglect or rejection. It learned to suppress emotional needs to avoid getting hurt again, builds walls and defenses to protect against more pain, and often acts tough or independent to hide vulnerability.

The problem is that these two parts are constantly in conflict within the person. The Needing Self wants to reach out and connect, while the Rejected Self cautions against it, warning "Don't bother, they'll just hurt again." This creates constant internal tension and emotional instability. This divided self affects more than just psychology - it impacts a person's identity, self-esteem, and even their spiritual life.

Kirwin connects the divided self to the development of personality disorders, especially Reactive Attachment Disorder. RAD typically develops from severe disruptions in early attachments, such as neglect, abuse, prolonged separations from caregivers, or inconsistent care from multiple caregivers as often happens in foster care situations.

Kirwin also points out that these early disruptions extend beyond psychological problems—they affect spiritual life as well. People with a divided self often struggle to trust in faith or God, feel part of a community, believe in unconditional love, or open themselves to spiritual experiences. Why? Because these abstract spiritual concepts require the same kind of trust that was never learned in human relationships. If someone couldn't trust their parents to be present for them, how can they trust an invisible God?

CONCLUSION

Early attachment experiences aren't merely events of the past—they actively shape who individuals are in the present. From Bowlby's discovery of the three separation phases to Kirwin's insights about the divided self, research clearly demonstrates that caregiving has a profound impact on trust, intimacy, and self-perception.

When caregivers are secure, consistent, and responsive, they create a strong foundation for healthy relationship patterns that last a lifetime. However, when attachment is disrupted or insufficient, it can leave lasting wounds that manifest as difficulty managing emotions, confusing and contradictory feelings in relationships, and psychological disorders such as Reactive Attachment Disorder.

The encouraging news is that understanding these patterns represents the first step toward healing. Even if secure attachment wasn't received as a child, new patterns can be learned, and healthier relationships can be built.

In the next chapter, the discussion will delve deeper into Reactive Attachment Disorder and other specific attachment-related challenges, exploring what they look like and how they can be addressed.

CHAPTER 3: REACTIVE ATTACHMENT DISORDER (RAD)

Imagine a child who either pushes everyone away or clings to complete strangers. Both behaviors might seem completely opposite, but they can stem from the same problem: Reactive Attachment Disorder, or RAD for short.

RAD is a serious condition that shows up in early childhood when children struggle to form healthy attachments, especially with their parents or main caregivers. It's usually caused by family problems, separation, abuse, or neglect, and it typically becomes obvious before a child turns five. RAD deeply affects how a child develops socially and emotionally, leading to behaviors that can cause problems throughout their entire life.

The official psychology guidebook, the DSM-IV, identifies two main types of RAD: Inhibitive RAD and Disinhibitive RAD. Each type looks very different on the outside, but both come from the same root problem—broken early attachments.

TYPE 1: INHIBITIVE RAD (THE "PUSH EVERYONE AWAY" TYPE)

What It Looks Like

Inhibitive RAD occurs when children avoid social interactions and have extreme difficulty forming relationships with anyone—peers, adults, even their own parents. This isn't just being shy. Shy children eventually warm up to people. Children with Inhibitive RAD stay withdrawn no matter what, and it affects every part of their social life.

These children might appear emotionally detached or "cold," not seek comfort from caregivers even when they're clearly upset or scared, struggle to form any meaningful connections, and seem unresponsive to people trying to connect with them.

Key Behaviors to Watch For

Complete Social Withdrawal

Children with Inhibitive RAD consistently avoid interactions with both peers and adults, even in places where they should feel safe, like home or school. Unlike shy children who eventually warm up, they maintain their distance across all settings. They isolate themselves during group activities, prefer to stay unnoticed and alone, and won't engage even in familiar, comfortable environments.

Won't Seek Comfort

Most children run to their parents when they're hurt, scared, or upset. Not these children. They don't reach out for comfort even when they're clearly distressed. They act stoic or detached when one would expect them to be emotional. They avoid eye contact, resist physical touch like hugs, and show signs of emotional disengagement. This isn't because they don't feel pain or fear—they've simply learned that reaching out doesn't help.

Emotional Detachment

This is the hallmark sign. These children seem indifferent or apathetic about everything. They appear unresponsive to both positive and negative situations, joylessness during celebrations like birthdays and holidays, and unemotional during sad moments such as losses or disappointments. People often misunderstand this as a child lacking emotion, but it's actually a defense mechanism. They've shut down emotionally to protect themselves from being hurt again.

Fear of Depending on Others

These children often display extreme independence because they deeply distrust caregivers or authority figures. They refuse help even when they clearly need it, act hyper-independent, won't rely on anyone for anything, and see asking for help as dangerous.

Suppressed Emotional Needs

In environments where expressing needs didn't result in care, these children adapted by suppressing those needs entirely. They learned that if they cry, no one comes anyway, so why bother. They learned that needing people only leads to disappointment and that they have to take care of themselves.

Avoiding Affection

Physical and emotional affection—even when it's appropriate and loving—gets met with avoidance or resistance. They might pull away from hugs, stiffen when touched, reject expressions of love, and seem uncomfortable with normal displays of affection.

What Causes Inhibitive RAD?

History of Neglect

These children often came from environments where their basic emotional or physical needs weren't consistently met. They learned that expressing needs doesn't lead to comfort, which reinforced their avoidance behaviors.

Chronic Stress or Trauma

Living with domestic violence, parental substance abuse, frequent changes in caregivers, or unpredictable and unsafe environments disrupts the development of secure attachments. Children learn to suppress emotional responses just to survive.

Institutional Care Settings

Studies show that children raised in orphanages or group homes, especially those with high caregiver-to-child ratios, are at higher risk for Inhibitive RAD. When consistent, individualized care isn't provided, emotional withdrawal becomes a protective mechanism.

Inconsistent Caregiving

When caregivers alternate between being attentive and neglectful, it creates confusion and insecurity. The child never knows what to expect, so they stop expecting anything at all and avoid relationships entirely.

The Long-Term Impact

If Inhibitive RAD goes untreated, the effects can last a lifetime. In terms of social development, individuals experience extreme difficulty forming and keeping friendships, appearing isolated or completely uninterested in others, experiencing deep loneliness, and finding themselves unable to integrate into social groups.

Regarding emotional health, they face difficulty understanding or processing emotions, both their own and others'. They experience challenges with empathy and problems with emotional intimacy throughout life.

Academic struggles often emerge as social withdrawal and emotional issues negatively affect school performance. Teachers often misinterpret their behavior as laziness or defiance, which creates more problems on top of existing issues.

For future relationships, without treatment, individuals struggle to form secure relationships as adults. Romantic partnerships prove especially difficult, and they may perpetuate a cycle of isolation and disconnection.

TYPE 2: DISINHIBITIVE RAD (THE "TOO FRIENDLY WITH STRANGERS" TYPE)

What It Looks Like

Disinhibitive RAD is the complete opposite of Inhibitive RAD. While Inhibitive children push everyone away, Disinhibitive children are overly friendly—especially with strangers. They form superficial relationships with anyone and everyone, showing no appropriate caution or boundaries.

Key Behaviors to Watch For

Excessive Friendliness with Strangers

Children with Disinhibitive RAD show unusual eagerness to engage with people they don't know. This includes excessive physical affection with strangers, no concept of personal boundaries, openly seeking attention or comfort from people they just met, and acting like everyone is their best friend.

Superficial Charm

These children often appear engaging and friendly on the surface, but their interactions lack genuine depth. The warmth seems fake or rehearsed. There's no real emotional connection behind their friendliness, it's all surface-level.

Can't Form Close Relationships

Here's the irony: despite being extremely social with strangers, they struggle to form secure attachments with the people who matter most—their caregivers, parents, and family members. This points to a fundamental problem in how they attach to people.

Inappropriate Attachments

These children might form attachments that are far too intense and far too fast. They treat strangers they just met like close family members and become vulnerable to exploitation or harm because they trust everyone indiscriminately.

Social Impulsivity
They fail to assess risks or understand social norms. They might hug complete strangers, share personal or family information with anyone, fail to recognize dangerous situations, and demonstrate no filter or caution in their social interactions.

What Causes Disinhibitive RAD?

Inconsistent Caregiving
When care is unpredictable, sometimes attentive, sometimes neglectful, children can't develop trust. They learn to seek attachment wherever they can find it as a survival mechanism.

Frequent Changes in Caregivers
Situations like foster care with multiple placements, institutional living, frequent relocation, and multiple caregivers moving in and out of their life disrupt the continuity needed for secure attachment. Children never learn to distinguish between familiar and unfamiliar people.

Neglect and Abuse
Early experiences of neglect or abuse teach children that their primary caregivers are unreliable or untrustworthy, so they look for care anywhere they can get it.

Institutionalization
Children raised in orphanages are especially vulnerable to Disinhibitive RAD because of the lack of individualized attention, absence of stable relationships, and high turnover of staff. Research consistently shows that institutionalized children develop indiscriminate friendliness as a way to cope.

Regarding social vulnerability, individuals face a heightened risk of exploitation or harm. Their overly trusting behavior makes them targets for dangerous situations, especially as they get older.

For relationship challenges, their superficial charm makes it hard to form deep, meaningful connections. They experience feelings of loneliness or rejection as they realize their relationships are hollow.

Emotionally, they struggle with difficulty regulating emotions, impulsive actions, and trouble understanding appropriate emotional responses.

Educational issues emerge as impulsivity and lack of boundaries lead to behavioral problems at school, disciplinary actions, and poor academic performance.

Mental health risks include a higher likelihood of developing anxiety, depression, or conduct disorders later in life.

A MORE DETAILED LOOK: DR. ZEANAH'S FRAMEWORK

Since RAD was first added to the official psychology manual, the DSM-III, research has expanded considerably. Dr. Charles Zeanah, a leading researcher in child psychiatry, proposed a more detailed way of understanding attachment disorders. His framework demonstrates that attachment problems are more complex than just the two DSM categories. He identified three main types.

Non-Attached Children

These children can't form attachments to any caregiver. This category breaks down into two subtypes. Indiscriminate Sociability describes children who are overly social with everyone, approaching all people with the same familiarity and ignoring social boundaries. This is similar to Disinhibitive RAD. Emotional Withdrawal describes children who demonstrate a lack of responsiveness, emotional withdrawal, and little interest in connecting with others, similar to Inhibitive RAD.

Disordered Attachments

These children have attachments, but they're unhealthy or maladaptive. They can't use caregivers as a secure base for exploration. Subtypes include those with inhibition, who show excessive clinginess and dependency on caregivers to the point where it interferes with normal development. Those with self-endangerment lack safety-seeking behavior. These children don't recognize danger or seek protection in threatening situations. Those with role reversal take on caregiving roles, prioritizing their caregiver's emotional needs over their own. This is especially sad—imagine a five-year-old trying to take care of their parent's emotions.

Disrupted Attachments

This occurs when a child experiences significant loss or separation from their primary caregiver. It triggers a grief-like response that leads to profound attachment difficulties. Long-term consequences include an inability to trust and difficulty forming close relationships.

WHAT CAUSES RAD? THE BIG PICTURE

RAD is tied to early-life experiences that disrupt the development of secure attachments. Neglect occurs when caregivers fail to meet a child's basic physical and emotional needs over a long period of time. Abuse, whether physical, emotional, or sexual, disrupts the child's sense of safety and trust—both essential for forming secure attachments. Institutionalization means that children in orphanages or foster care with high caregiver turnover lack consistent emotional support. Family separation involves long separations due to incarceration, illness, deployment, or other circumstances that prevent attachment from developing.

LONG-TERM PSYCHOLOGICAL PROBLEMS

Without treatment, RAD can have lasting effects on mental health and social functioning. Research shows that children with RAD are at higher risk of developing Borderline Personality Disorder, characterized by emotional instability, fear of abandonment, and serious relationship difficulties—all linked to early attachment disruptions. They face increased risk of anxiety and depression, as chronic emotional neglect leads to persistent sadness, hopelessness, and fear. RAD is sometimes associated with conduct disorders, including sociopathic behaviors such as manipulation and lack of empathy.

WHAT HAPPENS IN THE BRAIN?

Neuroscience research has revealed how early attachment disruptions physically affect brain development. Chronic neglect or abuse during critical developmental periods can actually alter brain structures involved in emotional regulation, social functioning, and empathy. Specifically, areas like the amygdala, which serves as the emotion center, and the prefrontal cortex, responsible for decision-making and impulse control, can be changed. These physical brain changes impair a person's ability to manage emotions, empathize with others, and form healthy relationships.

HOW IS RAD DIAGNOSED?

Diagnosing RAD requires a comprehensive evaluation by mental health professionals, which typically involves clinical interviews—detailed conversations with caregivers to understand the child's early experiences and behavior patterns. It includes behavioral observation, watching how the child interacts in various settings such as home, school, and social situations. Professionals also use standardized assessment tools like the Strange Situation Procedure, which was discussed in Chapter 1, or the Child Behavior Checklist to identify attachment issues.

TREATMENT FOR RAD

The encouraging news is that RAD can be treated. Effective treatment focuses on creating a stable, nurturing environment and addressing the child's emotional and relational needs. Common interventions include several approaches.

Therapeutic parenting involves training caregivers to provide consistent care, responsive attention to the child's needs, and empathetic interactions.

Attachment-based therapy, such as Dyadic Developmental Psychotherapy or DDP, strengthens the caregiver-child bond by addressing past trauma, fostering trust, and building healthy attachment patterns.

Play therapy uses structured play sessions to help children express emotions they can't verbalize, develop healthier ways of relating to others, and work through trauma in a safe, age-appropriate way.

Trauma-Focused Cognitive Behavioral Therapy, known as TF-CBT, addresses the impact of early trauma, emotional regulation problems, and maladaptive behaviors.

CHALLENGES IN TREATING RAD

Treating RAD is incredibly difficult. Several main challenges emerge in the therapeutic process.

Establishing Trust

One of the biggest obstacles is that people with RAD deeply distrust others, especially authority figures or caregivers. They experience a fear of vulnerability because they associate closeness with pain or rejection, so they resist opening up to therapists or caregivers. This can be manifested as avoidance, defiance, or manipulation. They demonstrate resistance to authority because adults in authority positions were often the source of their trauma. They struggle to distinguish between safe and unsafe authority figures. This mistrust extends to therapists, teachers, and mentors. For those exploring faith-based healing, this lack of trust can extend to how they relate to God as a father figure. If their human caregivers weren't trustworthy, how can they trust an invisible God? Therapists need to employ creative strategies to build trust, and it takes considerable time. Patience and persistence are essential.

Emotional Dysregulation

People with RAD struggle to regulate their emotions because they didn't have stable emotional support during their formative years. This manifests as outbursts and aggression—frequent temper tantrums, aggression, or destructive behavior that disrupts therapy sessions. Many experience difficulty expressing emotions and can't identify or articulate their feelings, a condition called alexithymia. This makes talk therapy extremely challenging. They also demonstrate fear of emotional closeness, meaning even well-meaning gestures from therapists or caregivers might be met with resistance or hostility. Therapists use techniques like mindfulness exercises, somatic therapy, or EMDR—Eye Movement Desensitization and Reprocessing—to help address these challenges.

Deep-Rooted Attachment Patterns

RAD stems from disrupted early attachment patterns, which are incredibly hard to change. Early experiences create mental "blueprints" for relationships called internal working models. For people with RAD, these blueprints emphasize self-reliance and distrust, making it hard to accept help. Children might show confusing behaviors like indiscriminate affection with strangers or total emotional withdrawal that confuse caregivers and therapists. These patterns developed early and were reinforced over time, making them resistant to change. Efforts to challenge them may be met with defensiveness or regression. Treatment requires consistency, patience, and repeated positive experiences to reshape these mental blueprints.

Trauma and PTSD

RAD often comes with post-traumatic stress disorder or PTSD, which complicates treatment. Individuals experience hypervigilance, constantly scanning for threats and unable to relax or engage meaningfully in therapy. They suffer from flashbacks where past trauma intrudes on the present, causing distress during therapy sessions. They may practice avoidance, steering clear of certain topics, environments, or people to cope with trauma, which limits therapy's effectiveness. Trauma-informed care is essential. Techniques like TF-CBT or EMDR help people process trauma safely.

Family Dynamics

Treatment involves not just the individual but also their family or caregiving environment. Problems include caregiver burnout, as caring for someone with RAD is exhausting and frustrating. Burned-out caregivers can't provide the consistent, empathetic care needed for recovery. Inconsistent parenting emerges when multiple caregivers use different approaches, which worsens RAD symptoms. Sibling resentment may develop as siblings feel neglected because the child with RAD requires so much attention. Family therapy and caregiver training are critical components of RAD treatment.

Cultural and Social Barriers

In many cultures, mental health conditions carry significant stigmas. Families may delay seeking help due to fear of judgment. Limited access to services means many areas lack specialized mental health services, especially rural or underserved communities. Cultural differences in parenting styles complicate matters, as what's considered neglectful in one context might not be in another, complicating diagnosis and treatment. Culturally sensitive approaches are essential.

Adolescence and Adulthood

Although RAD is diagnosed in early childhood, its effects often persist. Challenges include the development of unhealthy coping mechanisms like substance abuse, self-harm, or compulsive behaviors to manage unresolved pain. Interpersonal difficulties arise as the inability to form secure attachments leads to problems in romantic relationships, friendships, and work. Comorbid disorders present a higher risk, including anxiety, depression, or personality disorders. Adolescents and adults may need intensive interventions including individual therapy, group therapy, and support networks.

PREVENTING RAD

Prevention requires early intervention and support for at-risk families. Parenting education teaches caregivers the skills to meet their child's emotional and developmental needs. Support services provide resources like counseling, financial assistance, and parenting programs to families in crisis. Early identification through screening for attachment issues in high-risk settings such as foster care and orphanages allows for timely help.

ETHICAL CONCERNS

Some controversial treatments for RAD have been used in the past, like "holding therapy," which involves physically restraining the child to elicit emotional responses. Many professional organizations, including the American Academy of

Child and Adolescent Psychiatry, strongly oppose these practices because they can cause harm, lack scientific evidence of effectiveness, and may retraumatize already-traumatized children.

WHAT WE STILL NEED TO LEARN

While much has been learned about RAD, gaps remain. Future research should focus on longitudinal studies that follow children with RAD into adulthood to observe long-term outcomes. Research needs to determine intervention effectiveness by figuring out which therapeutic approaches work best for different populations. Understanding cultural factors and how cultural differences influence attachment formation and RAD expression remains important.

CONCLUSION

Reactive Attachment Disorder is a complex condition rooted in early attachment disruptions. It has far-reaching effects on emotional, social, and psychological well-being. Understanding RAD requires knowledge from psychology, neuroscience, and social work.

Treating RAD presents many challenges - from establishing trust to addressing deep trauma and navigating systemic barriers. But these obstacles aren't insurmountable. With a compassionate, multifaceted approach to care, therapists, biblical counselors, caregivers, and communities can provide the support needed to help people with RAD move toward healing and growth.

The key to understanding is that early attachments matter profoundly. When they're disrupted, the consequences without intervention can last a lifetime. But with proper understanding, support, and treatment, healing is possible.

CHAPTER 4: HOW PARENTS SHAPE WHO INDIVIDUALS BECOME

Parents, especially fathers, play a huge role in shaping how individuals connect with people throughout their lives. The way parents treat their children as babies and young children creates patterns that persist into adulthood, often without conscious awareness.

John Bowlby and other researchers demonstrated that babies aren't born as blank slates. They're constantly learning from how their caregivers treat them. This influence is especially powerful in the early years, when consistent caregiving shapes emotions, behavior, and personality. When things go wrong during this critical time, it doesn't just affect human relationships—it can even impact spiritual life and how individuals relate to God.

This chapter explores how early caregiving experiences, particularly with fathers, deeply impact how people form attachments, their personality development, and their spiritual connections. The chapter also introduces a concept called Spiritual Attachment Disorder, or SAD, which explores the connection between early attachment experiences and the ability to form a secure relationship with God or a higher power.

HOW PARENTS INFLUENCE ATTACHMENT

Bowlby explained that attachment is an instinct—babies are born with a built-in system designed to keep them close to their caregivers for survival. These early experiences with caregivers become templates or blueprints for all future relationships.

The pattern works like this: consistent, responsive caregiving leads to secure attachment patterns, while disrupted or absent caregiving leads to insecure attachment patterns. These patterns have far-reaching consequences for emotional health and relationships throughout life.

THE UNIQUE ROLE OF FATHERS

While much research has focused on mothers, and their role will be discussed as well, researchers have recently been paying more attention to fathers. Fathers contribute uniquely to a child's development in ways that complement what mothers provide. Fathers shape emotional, behavioral, and even spiritual growth in distinct ways.

Emotional Support and Being Available

When fathers are emotionally present and attentive, they provide a "secure base" from which children can explore the world. Research by Lamb in 2010 found that children who experience emotional support from their fathers have better emotional regulation, meaning they can manage their feelings more effectively. They show more resilience, bouncing back from setbacks more readily. They feel more confident exploring and taking healthy risks. When children know their father has their back, they're more willing to try new things because they're not afraid of failing.

Modeling How Relationships Work

Fathers serve as role models for how relationships should work. They influence how children understand authority and what healthy leadership looks like. They shape perceptions of trust, teaching when and how to trust others. They model emotional connection and demonstrate how to be close to someone. Studies by Grossmann and colleagues in 2002 emphasize that fathers play a special role in encouraging independence and exploration, which balances out the mother's traditionally nurturing role. This gives children a well-rounded view of relationships.

Spiritual Leadership

In many families, fathers act as spiritual guides, shaping how children understand God and faith. Here's something particularly important: children often project their understanding of their earthly father onto their concept of God. For example, if a father is loving, present, and trustworthy, children are more likely to see God as loving, present, and trustworthy. Conversely, if a father is absent, harsh, or unpredictable, children might struggle to trust God or see Him as distant and harsh. This connection between earthly fathers and views of God represents one of the most powerful influences on spiritual life.

THE MOTHER'S CORRESPONDING ROLE

While this chapter focuses on fathers, mothers play an equally vital role that shouldn't be overlooked. Mothers traditionally serve as primary caregivers, providing the nurturing and consistent care that forms the foundation of secure attachments. Their presence in early development helps establish emotional stability, social bonding skills, and relational trust.

What Makes Mothers So Important?

Research by Mary Ainsworth, whose Strange Situation experiment was discussed earlier, highlights something called "maternal sensitivity" as a major predictor of secure attachment. Maternal sensitivity means noticing and accurately responding to a child's emotional and physical needs, responding to cries promptly, understanding non-verbal cues such as when a baby is tired or overstimulated, and providing comfort during distress. Children with sensitive mothers are much more likely to develop secure attachment patterns. All of these maternal behaviors promote a child's sense of safety and trust.

Teaching Emotional Regulation

Mothers play a critical role in teaching children how to manage their emotions. Through consistent care, they help children learn to understand their feelings, express emotions in healthy ways, and self-soothe when upset. For example, when a child is upset, a nurturing mother provides comfort and reassurance. Over time, this teaches the child how to calm themselves down. This builds emotional resilience—the ability to cope with stress and navigate complex social situations.

Building Empathy

Maternal behaviors significantly influence the development of empathy. By modeling compassionate and nurturing interactions, mothers teach children to recognize other people's emotions, respond appropriately to others' feelings, and care about how their actions affect others. Empathy is a cornerstone of healthy relationships, and it stems from these early lessons in emotional understanding.

Role Models for Closeness and Intimacy

Mothers serve as primary role models for relational intimacy and nurturing behaviors. They demonstrate how to build trust, maintain open communication, and express affection in healthy ways. These lessons extend beyond family relationships. They influence how children interact with friends, romantic partners, and their own future children. A mother's ability to balance firmness with warmth gives children the tools to establish meaningful and secure connections throughout life.

The Perfect Team: Fathers and Mothers Together

While fathers often encourage autonomy and exploration, essentially saying "Go ahead, try it," mothers typically provide a secure base to return to, communicating "I'm here if you need me." This complementary dynamic ensures that children benefit from a balanced approach to emotional and cognitive development.

For example, a father might inspire a child to take risks and try new things, while a mother offers the emotional grounding necessary to process failures or setbacks. Together, these roles create a strong foundation for personal growth and resilience.

HOW CULTURE AFFECTS PARENTAL ROLES

The way parents influence attachment is deeply connected to culture. Different societies have different expectations for mothers and fathers.

Traditional Societies

In many patriarchal societies, fathers are seen as authority figures and providers, mothers take on primary caregiving responsibilities, and spiritual guidance often falls to fathers as moral and spiritual leaders. In these settings, mothers are viewed as the emotional heart of the family, fostering close bonds and teaching values like cooperation and empathy. Their influence on attachment is especially pronounced because they spend so much time with children during formative years.

Modern Societies

The way society thinks about parenting roles has evolved in contemporary cultures. There's now a more equal distribution of responsibilities between mothers and fathers. Dual-career households mean both parents often work. Shared parenting initiatives emphasize both parents' involvement in caregiving. Fathers are more involved in day-to-day emotional care. This shift doesn't diminish the importance of either parent—it highlights the benefits of collaborative parenting. When both parents are actively involved, children experience diverse emotional, cognitive, and social experiences, which enhances their adaptability and relationship skills.

Different Cultures, Same Goal

Research by Keller in 2018 shows how cultural norms influence attachment formation. In collectivist cultures, such as many Asian and Latin American societies, mothers often emphasize family unity and communal responsibilities. The focus is on being part of a group. In individualist cultures, like the United States and Western Europe, mothers may encourage independence while still being emotionally available. The focus is on becoming one's own person. Despite these differences, the underlying goal remains the same across all cultures: fostering secure attachments that help children thrive.

ATTACHMENT PATTERNS GET PASSED DOWN THROUGH GENERATIONS

Here's something fascinating and somewhat concerning: attachment styles often get passed down from parents to children through parenting behaviors and relationship patterns. Children of securely attached parents are more likely to develop secure attachments themselves, while children of insecurely attached parents face a higher risk of attachment challenges.

How Does This Happen?

Modeling Behaviors

Parents unconsciously model relationship behaviors based on their own attachment histories. For example, a securely attached mother demonstrates consistent caregiving, and her child learns to do the same. A securely attached father models what a good husband looks like, showing his daughter what to look for in a future partner and teaching his son how to be a good father someday.

Parenting Practices

Parents' attachment styles influence how they discipline their children, provide emotional support, and handle conflicts. For instance, an anxiously attached mother may be overprotective, not giving her child enough independence. An avoidant-attached mother may appear emotionally distant, not providing enough warmth. These parenting approaches then shape the child's attachment style.

Breaking the Cycle

The encouraging news is that the cycle of insecure attachment can be broken. It requires intentional reflection and action, but it's entirely possible. Parents who recognize their own attachment challenges can seek therapy or pastoral counseling to address unresolved issues. They can practice conscious parenting by prioritizing emotional availability. They can foster open communication with their children and work on their own issues so they don't pass them on to the next generation. By doing this work, individuals can create secure attachment patterns in the next generation, even if they didn't have them themselves.

HOW THIS AFFECTS SPIRITUAL LIFE

A father's spiritual leadership is incredibly important in children's development, and a mother's nurturing role also impacts spiritual growth significantly. A child's first experience of unconditional love comes through maternal caregiving. This experience shapes how they understand their relationship with God.

Securely attached individuals are more likely to view God as loving, trustworthy, present, and caring. People with insecure attachments may struggle with feeling spiritually alienated, fearing God rather than loving Him, viewing God as distant or unreliable, and experiencing difficulty trusting in God's love. This makes sense when one considers that if an earthly father was harsh and unpredictable, an individual might imagine God the Father the same way. If a mother's love felt conditional, someone might struggle to believe in God's unconditional love.

Practical Applications for Parents and Churches

Faith-Based Parenting

Parents can be encouraged to adopt practices that model unconditional love, trustworthiness, consistency, and grace and forgiveness. These approaches can foster spiritual security in children.

Pastoral Counseling

Churches can provide pastoral counseling to address attachment-related spiritual challenges. This can help people reconcile the influence of their parents with their faith.

Spiritual Growth Programs

Faith communities can develop programs that emphasize healing from past wounds, restoration of broken relationships, and integrating early attachment experiences with one's spiritual journey. These programs allow individuals to heal and grow spiritually despite difficult early experiences.

CONCLUSION

Parents, especially fathers but mothers as well, have a lasting influence on how individuals form attachments, their emotional development, and their spiritual connections. While early experiences set the stage for relationship and spiritual patterns, the encouraging news is that these patterns can be reshaped. Through therapy, pastoral counseling, and intentional spiritual growth, individuals can heal and develop new, healthier patterns. Understanding the powerful connection between parental roles and attachment helps illuminate why nurturing caregiving is so important. It affects not just childhood but relationships, emotional health, and spiritual life for an entire lifetime.

The patterns parents create in their children don't have to be permanent. With understanding, support, and intentional effort, individuals can break negative cycles, develop secure attachment patterns, form healthy relationships, and connect with God in a deep, meaningful way.

Whether someone is a parent trying to do better for their children or working through their own attachment issues, the message is clear: change is possible, healing is available, and growth is always within reach.

CHAPTER 5: HOW CHILDHOOD AFFECTS ONE'S RELATIONSHIP WITH GOD

Here's something that might surprise many people: the way parents treated their children doesn't just affect human relationships—it also shapes how individuals relate to God. Research increasingly shows a powerful connection between early attachment experiences and spiritual development. Attachment theory, discussed in earlier chapters, was originally developed to explain the bonds between children and caregivers. But it turns out those same patterns also shape spiritual beliefs and practices later in life.

The basic pattern works like this: secure attachment leads to a trusting, positive view of God, while insecure attachment leads to skepticism, fear, or feeling disconnected from God. This chapter explores how early childhood experiences influence spiritual life and what can be done when early experiences weren't optimal.

WHAT RESEARCH TELLS US

Researchers Granqvist and Kirkpatrick conducted important studies in 2004 exploring how attachment experiences influence how people view God and engage in spiritual practices. Their findings reveal distinct patterns tied to different attachment styles.

People with Secure Attachment

If individuals had secure attachment as children—meaning they experienced warmth, consistency, and emotional availability from their caregivers—they're more likely to perceive God as loving and forgiving, reflecting the reliability and nurturing they experienced. They tend to see God as accessible and trustworthy, similar to the secure base their caregivers provided, and as present and caring, just as their parents were there when needed. This secure attachment creates a deep sense of spiritual connection. People with secure attachment often engage regularly in faith practices such as prayer, church attendance, and Bible study. They have a positive outlook on their relationship with God, find it relatively easy to trust Him, and feel comfortable approaching God with their problems. If parents were consistently loving and available, it makes sense that individuals would expect God to be the same way.

People with Insecure Attachment

If individuals experience inconsistency or neglect in their caregiver relationships, they often carry those same patterns into their spiritual life. People with insecure attachment tend to perceive God as distant or unresponsive, mirroring caregivers who weren't always available. They may view Him as punitive or judgmental, reflecting fears from inconsistent relationships, as unpredictable, never knowing if He'll be there, and as conditional in His love, believing they have to earn it just as they felt they had to earn their parents' attention.

These perceptions lead to struggles with trust and intimacy in both human and spiritual relationships. Individuals might have trouble praying because they don't think God is listening, feel like they have to be perfect for God to love them, struggle to believe God really cares about their problems, or feel spiritually distant even when trying to be close to God.

People with Avoidant Attachment

Avoidant attachment occurs when early caregiver unavailability taught individuals to be emotionally distant and self-reliant. People with avoidant attachment often view spiritual practices as irrelevant or untrustworthy, dismissing the need for a higher power. They consider them secondary to self-sufficiency, thinking they don't need God and can handle things themselves. Getting close to God feels like unnecessary emotional vulnerability and thus risky.

These individuals may avoid deeper spiritual exploration, engage only superficially with faith-based activities by going through the motions, and reflect a broader pattern of emotional detachment in all relationships, including with God.

THE GOOD NEWS: ATTACHMENT PATTERNS CAN CHANGE

Here's the most important thing to understand, while attachment styles have profound effects on spiritual development, they are not fixed. John Bowlby, the founder of attachment theory, emphasized that attachment patterns can be reshaped through intentional efforts.

Even if individuals had terrible early experiences, they can develop a healthy relationship with God and with other people. It takes work, but it's possible. There are two main ways people change their attachment patterns.

OPTION 1: THERAPEUTIC INTERVENTIONS

Therapy offers a structured approach to addressing attachment wounds and healing relationships.

Attachment-Based Therapy

Approaches like Emotionally Focused Therapy, or EFT, and Dyadic Developmental Psychotherapy, known as DDP, focus on repairing early relational trauma, fostering secure attachments, emphasizing emotional connection, and helping individuals rebuild trust in relationships. When people rebuild trust in human relationships through therapy, this often extends to their spiritual life as well. As they learn to trust their therapist and work through their issues, they may find it easier to trust God.

Narrative Therapy

This type of therapy helps individuals reframe their life story. For example, someone might view their caregiver as neglectful. Through therapy, they come to understand the circumstances that shaped their caregiver's behavior, perhaps they were dealing with depression, addiction, or their own trauma. This understanding fosters compassion and reduces resentment. They realize their caregiver's failings weren't about them being unlovable. By recontextualizing past attachment experiences, individuals can release some of the pain and move forward with healthier patterns.

OPTION 2: SPIRITUAL INTERVENTIONS

Spiritual practices can work alongside therapy or offer an alternative path to relational and emotional healing.

Guided Spiritual Practices

Activities like prayer, Bible study, and meditation can help individuals understand God better as they release their fears to Him, allow Him to intervene in their lives, experience His presence and love directly, and gradually reshape their view of who God is. For example, spending time reading about God's character in Scripture can challenge false beliefs developed from childhood experiences. If someone grew up thinking love is conditional, verses about God's unconditional love can slowly reshape that belief.

Community Support

Engaging with faith communities such as local churches provide relational healing through supportive networks. Shared worship creates a sense of belonging. Communal activities provide healthy relationship experiences. Mentorship within church groups helps rebuild trust. Individuals experience unconditional love that may have been absent in early relationships. Sometimes, experiencing consistent love and acceptance from a church community can model what healthy relationships look like, which then changes how people relate to God.

SPIRITUAL ATTACHMENT DISORDER

Some people walk through life with an unseen barrier that prevents them from forming any spiritual relationship with God. From a psychological viewpoint, this is called Spiritual Attachment Disorder, or SAD. Spiritual Attachment Disorder refers to the inability to form a secure spiritual connection, often mirroring patterns of insecure human attachments.

SAD manifests in several ways. First, there's avoidance of spiritual connection, where individuals reject or avoid spiritual practices entirely, view them as unreliable or unnecessary, feel uncomfortable with anything related to faith, or dismiss spiritual experiences as fake or emotional manipulation.

Second, there's fear of abandonment by God, which mirrors anxious attachment styles. Individuals constantly worry that

God will abandon them, feel like they must perform perfectly or God will leave, and never feel secure in God's love, always anxious about losing it.

Third, there's perception of God as punitive, where individuals view God as harsh, judgmental, or angry, expect punishment rather than love, project negative paternal experiences onto God, and find it impossible to believe in a loving, graceful God. This will be explored in much more detail in Chapter 11.

SAD is a serious barrier to spiritual growth and peace. But like other attachment issues, it can be addressed and healed.

THE ROLE OF MEDIATORS IN HEALING

Researcher Alice Chornesky highlighted in 2012 the importance of mediators in addressing destructive attachment patterns. Mediators are people who act as bridges, helping individuals confront and reshape their perceptions of caregiving figures. Mediators can be therapists, pastors, mentors, spiritual counselors, trusted friends or family members, or small group leaders. These people help process experiences, challenge false beliefs, and develop healthier patterns.

Six Key Factors That Influence Parent-Child Relationships
Chornesky identified six key factors that affect parent-adult-child relationships. Understanding these can help identify where problems developed.

Family structure involves the composition and dynamics of one's family, which influence attachment patterns and expectations from relationships. For example, growing up in a single-parent household versus a two-parent household versus living with grandparents creates different dynamics.

Patterns of contact refer to how often individuals interacted with their caregivers and the quality of those interactions, which shape emotional bonds. For instance, seeing one's father every day versus only on weekends, or whether one's mother was emotionally present when physically there, makes a significant difference.

Shared values concern whether one's values align or conflict with family values, which impacts the emotional quality of relationships. If a family highly values achievement but an individual is more creative or laid-back, they might have experienced conflict or felt like they didn't measure up.

Norms and expectations involve societal and familial norms that guide behavior and relational roles. Cultural expectations about respect, independence, emotional expression, or gender roles all influence how individuals relate to their parents.

Patterns of support refer to the availability and consistency of emotional or material support, which shape trust and security. Whether one could count on parents when help was needed, or if they were sometimes supportive and sometimes dismissive, significantly affects attachment.

Emotional quality of ties concerns the depth of emotional connection, which determines the strength and resilience of relationships. Whether individuals felt deeply connected to their parents or the relationship was more surface-level they shape attachment patterns.

Chornesky's findings, supported by research from Gunhild Hagestad in 1987, underscore the importance of identifying and intervening in negative attachment patterns to foster healthier relationships. By examining these six factors with a mediator such as a therapist, pastor, or mentor, individuals can identify where things went wrong, understand why they developed certain patterns, work on changing those patterns, and develop healthier relationships moving forward.

HOW THIS APPLIES TO LIFE

Understanding the connection between attachment and spirituality has practical implications for different groups of people.

For Those Struggling Spiritually

Individuals struggling spiritually might ask themselves what their early experiences with caregivers were like, how those experiences might be affecting their view of God, whether they're projecting their parents' characteristics onto God, and what false beliefs about God they might have developed from childhood.

Then they can take action by considering therapy to address attachment wounds, finding a trusted mentor or pastor to talk through these issues, joining a supportive faith community, spending time reading Scripture passages about God's character, especially ones that contradict false beliefs, and practicing prayer and meditation, even if it feels uncomfortable at first.

For Parents

Parents should remember how they treat their children shapes not just human relationships but spiritual life as well. Being consistent, loving, and emotionally available helps children develop a healthy view of God. While parental failures don't doom children, healing one's own attachment issues helps break negative cycles.

For Those in Ministry

Those in ministry should recognize that people's spiritual struggles often have roots in attachment issues. Some people's difficulty connecting with God isn't about lack of faith—it's about attachment wounds. Creating safe, consistent, loving church environments can provide healing experiences. Patience and understanding are crucial when working with people who have attachment-related spiritual struggles.

CONCLUSION

The relationship between attachment and spirituality demonstrates just how profound early relational experiences are. They shape not just how people relate to others but how they relate to God.

Secure attachment fosters trust in God, intimacy with God, active engagement in spiritual practices, and a generally positive spiritual life. Insecure attachment can result in skepticism about faith, fear of God or feeling distant from Him, avoidance of spiritual practices, and Spiritual Attachment Disorder.

But here's the most important understanding: attachment patterns are not unchangeable. Through therapeutic interventions such as professional counseling and spiritual interventions like faith-based healing practices, individuals can heal relational wounds, reshape their attachment style, and cultivate a deeper connection with themselves, others, and God. This dynamic interplay between attachment and spirituality highlights something truly hopeful: understanding attachment patterns gives people the power to change them. Individuals are not stuck with the patterns their childhood created. With effort, support, and intentionality, they can develop secure attachments and a deep, fulfilling relationship with God—no matter what their early experiences were like.

The journey might not be easy, but it's well worth it. The past doesn't have to define the future, and early wounds don't have to determine spiritual life. Healing is possible, growth is available, and a secure relationship with God is within reach.

CHAPTER 6: MEDIATORS AND BIBLICAL PRINCIPLES

In the previous chapter, six key factors that affect parent-child relationships were discussed. Now, these factors will be examined from a Biblical perspective—because for those approaching this from a faith standpoint, these factors need to align with spiritual principles.

CONNECTING PSYCHOLOGY TO FAITH

The six factors connect to spiritual life in meaningful ways. Family structure relates to understanding one's relationship with God as Father. Patterns of contact correspond to maintaining ongoing communication with God through prayer, worship, and the church family. Shared values and beliefs involve grounding oneself in God's Word, the Bible. Norms and expectations mean using Scripture as a guide for life. Patterns of support involve fostering a supportive faith community and addressing any barriers caused by sinful behaviors. Emotional ties concern building genuine intimacy with God.

The concept of mediation is central to Biblical counseling. The Bible presents Jesus as the ultimate mediator—the one who reconciles humanity with God. In this context, a counselor's role mirrors that of a mediator, helping people rebuild their spiritual and emotional attachments through a framework grounded in Biblical principles.

By connecting psychological attachment theories with their spiritual implications, a complete picture emerges of how early attachment patterns influence both relational and spiritual well-being.

NEW WAYS OF UNDERSTANDING ATTACHMENT

Attachment theory, started by John Bowlby and developed further by Mary Ainsworth, has continued to evolve as researchers explore the nuances of attachment behavior. Charles Zeanah made a notable contribution by introducing three distinct subcategories that address more complex attachment patterns.

Non-Attached

Non-attached children fail to form any meaningful attachment relationships. This is different from insecure attachment—these children don't form connections at all. They display complete emotional detachment, no trust in caregivers, inability to seek comfort from others, and act as though they don't need anyone at all.

This pattern is typically caused by severe neglect, abandonment, or prolonged isolation during early childhood, such as growing up in an orphanage with minimal human contact. Without help, non-attached children struggle with emotional regulation, meaning managing their feelings, empathy or understanding others' emotions, and establishing meaningful relationships later in life.

Disordered Attachment

Disordered attachment means dysfunctional attachment behaviors that deviate significantly from typical patterns. These children display confusing, contradictory, or maladaptive behaviors with their caregivers. This is particularly associated with Reactive Attachment Disorder, or RAD, or Disinhibited Social Engagement Disorder, known as DSED.

These children may show excessive clinginess, aggression, indiscriminate friendliness such as being overly friendly with strangers, avoidance, and behaviors that seem disjointed and inconsistent. This pattern typically stems from inconsistent caregiving, trauma, abuse, or children struggling to predict or respond to caregiver behaviors.

If not addressed, these behaviors persist into adulthood, causing difficulties with emotional intimacy, trust issues, and social functioning problems.

Disrupted Attachment

Disrupted attachment happens when an established attachment pattern is interrupted by external factors. Unlike non-attached children, these children had attachment but lost it due to life circumstances. They display grief, anxiety, regressive behaviors such as acting younger than their age, and attempts to cope with the loss.

This pattern is caused by parental death, divorce, or frequent changes in caregivers like multiple foster home placements. Early intervention is crucial to help these children re-establish secure attachments and prevent long-term emotional or relational challenges.

These findings reinforce how significant early life experiences are in shaping long-term emotional and social development.

CONNECTING FAMILY ISSUES TO BIBLICAL PRINCIPLES

Researcher Hagestad, building on Chornesky's work, identified six key family issues. Each of these has a direct connection to a Biblical principle.

Family structure corresponds to one's relationship with God as Father. Specific patterns of contact relate to an ongoing relationship through prayer, worship, times for praise, and seeking His will in one's life. Shared values and beliefs involve a specific time set apart for God's Word. Norms and expectations raise the question of whether God's Word serves as the measuring stick for one's life. Patterns of support address whether sinful behavior has brought distance between an individual and the Father, and whether that person is rooted in a Bible-believing fellowship of believers. Affective quality of ties recognizes that one can only experience intimacy with someone they're truly in love with.

This framework shows how psychological concepts and spiritual principles intersect. A person's relationship with their earthly father shapes their relationship with their Heavenly Father, and vice versa.

THE MODERN FAMILY CRISIS: CHORNESKY'S OBSERVATIONS

Researcher Chornesky examined the challenges faced by the nuclear family—mom, dad, and kids—in modern society. She emphasized that the family unit, historically a stable foundation of society, is undergoing significant changes. Central to this is the role of fathers, which is being reshaped in ways that some view as liberating but which Chornesky warned could actually destabilize families.

The Redefinition of Parental Roles

Modern culture has reinterpreted parental roles, particularly what fathers are supposed to do. This is often framed as fostering individual autonomy and equality among caregivers. However, Chornesky argued that such changes, while well-intentioned, may weaken the traditional family model by undermining the supportive and positively influential roles that parents, especially fathers, are meant to play.

She suggested that decades of cultural shifts have normalized this challenge to the family unit, contributing to an erosion of how effective fathers can be. Increased divorce rates, single-parent households becoming more common, cultural messages that fathers are optional or interchangeable, and media portrayals of dads as incompetent or unnecessary all contribute to this phenomenon.

Restoring paternal influence and repairing the damage from these shifts requires what Chornesky called a "mediator."

WHAT IS A MEDIATOR?

A mediator is someone who acts as a bridge to address earlier disruptions in caregiver relationships and attachment problems. The mediator helps restore the essential functions of parental caregiving within the family.

The Mediator's Role

Mediators play a transformative role by enabling people to reshape their perceptions of family relationships, particularly the father-child dynamic. This transformation happens through meaningful contact and emotional intimacy, which act as catalysts for change.

Patterns of Contact and Intimacy

When people experience meaningful interactions, these moments can reshape their life narratives and foster healthier relationship dynamics. For contact to work as an effective mediator, it must include positive communication, mutual respect, and a focus on shared values.

Shared Values and Beliefs

Chornesky argued that shared values and beliefs provide the foundation for developing mediator-based relationships, which promotes a "socialization process emanating from parent to child." In other words, when individuals and their parents share core values, it creates common ground for healing.

Affective Closeness

Chornesky found that emotional intimacy within the parent-child relationship significantly influences change. The perception of emotional intimacy, particularly from the child's perspective, emerged as a critical motivator for altering attachment patterns.

Earlier research by Levinson found that unresolved conflicts between fathers and sons often lead to alienation. But the alienation is driven more by the son's perception than by the father's actual actions. This suggests that fostering emotional intimacy can help reframe relationship dynamics, even when the father hasn't made major behavioral changes. Sometimes, just understanding a father's perspective or circumstances can shift one's entire view of the relationship.

TRANSFORMING PERCEPTIONS THROUGH MEDIATORS

Chornesky's research revealed something powerful: adults could shift their perceptions of their fathers through the intervention of an external mediator. This effectively restructured their views of the caregiver relationship. Importantly, this transformation wasn't triggered by extraordinary life events but rather by a gradual shift in perspective facilitated by the mediator's influence.

Two critical points emerge from this finding. First, early life experiences have a profound impact. Experiences with one's father deeply shape how that person sees him—and how they see God. This concept is supported by Bowlby and other attachment theorists. Second, mediators provide a practical mechanism for change. The intervention of a mediator offers a way to transform negative perceptions into more accurate and constructive views.

The Divine-Human Connection

Chornesky emphasized that the subconscious often conflates "Father" referring to the divine God and "father" referring to the human dad. This means that life experiences with one's dad shape spiritual perceptions. If someone had a harsh father, they might see God as harsh. If they had an absent father, they might see God as distant.

By restructuring one's view of their earthly father through a mediator, individuals also have the potential to transform their view of their Heavenly Father. This is why mediators are so important—they help heal both human and spiritual relationships.

WHO CAN BE A MEDIATOR?

Mediators can take various forms. They might be a therapist or counselor, a pastor or spiritual mentor, a trusted family friend, a support group leader, or sometimes even a sibling or other family member.

From a Biblical perspective, Jesus is the ultimate Mediator between humanity and God. But on a practical, day-to-day level, human mediators can facilitate healing by providing supportive exchanges between parents and children, performing compassionate acts, cultivating shared experiences that foster trust and emotional intimacy, and helping someone invite the ultimate Mediator, Jesus, into their life's challenges.

Practical examples of mediation include a counselor helping an adult understand why their father was emotionally distant, perhaps because he dealt with depression or his own trauma. A pastor might help someone see God's true character despite having had a harsh earthly father. A mentor can model healthy fatherhood for someone who never experienced it. A support group can provide a safe space to process father wounds.

Even from a secular viewpoint, acts such as providing financial support during hardship, offering sympathetic understanding, and demonstrating consistent commitment can serve as mediating factors in rebuilding fractured relationships.

PRACTICAL IMPLICATIONS

Chornesky's work underscores the importance of identifying and fostering mediators within families and broader social systems. For those struggling with father wounds or attachment issues, finding a mediator can be life-changing.

Individuals can begin by recognizing the need, acknowledging that early experiences may have shaped perceptions in unhealthy ways. Finding a mediator involves seeking out a therapist, pastor, mentor, or trusted person who can help process experiences. Being open to change means allowing the mediator to help see things from new perspectives. Working on both relationships involves intentionally healing one's view of their earthly father while also working on their relationship with their Heavenly Father. Finally, being patient recognizes that this process takes time. Transformation is gradual, not instant.

CONCLUSION

Chornesky's findings show that secular research aligns closely with solutions rooted in Biblical perspectives, particularly in addressing early disruptions in attachment and paternal caregiving. The role of the mediator offers a pathway for restoring broken family relationships, making it an essential tool for healing. Mediators provide a practical and relational mechanism for growth, offering hope for people seeking to overcome the challenges of disrupted or disordered attachments. Several key understandings emerge from this chapter. Early attachment experiences shape both human relationships and one's relationship with God. The six key family issues have direct Biblical parallels. Modern culture has contributed to the erosion of the father's role, creating more attachment problems. Mediators can help transform negative perceptions and heal broken relationships. Jesus is the ultimate Mediator, but human mediators play a crucial practical role. Change is possible through mediation, even if early experiences were very difficult. The next chapter will go deeper into the mediator's role, its practical applications, and how it aligns with Chornesky's findings. The exploration will examine how mediation can be used as a tool for fostering relational restoration within families, both human and spiritual.

The message is clear: no matter how broken early attachments were, healing is possible. Through the right mediators, both human and divine, individuals can reshape their perceptions, heal their wounds, and develop healthy relationships with both people and God.

CHAPTER 7: FIXING THE DAMAGE, HOW TO HEAL FROM ADVERSE CHILDHOOD EXPERIENCES

Since John Bowlby first demonstrated how important early childhood attachments are—and how damaging they can be when they go wrong—countless studies have confirmed his findings. When children experience disrupted or harmful relationships with their caregivers, it creates serious problems in forming healthy adult relationships, including intimate and emotional bonds.

This chapter explores the critical need to address and heal the outcomes of adverse childhood experiences, or ACEs, especially when these experiences make it difficult to form secure emotional and spiritual connections. The damage from harsh, abusive, or neglectful parenting is far-reaching, affecting emotional well-being, social skills, and spiritual identity. The role of mediators—people who help facilitate healing and restore relationships—becomes essential in addressing these outcomes.

THE LASTING IMPACT OF BROKEN ATTACHMENTS

When children experience neglect or harm from their caregivers, the effects ripple out into adulthood. Studies consistently show that early disruptions increase the likelihood of difficulties in forming healthy adult relationships, especially those requiring intimacy and trust.

For people whose early experiences were marked by inconsistency, rejection, or abuse, common struggles include emotional disconnection from others, a pervasive sense of being unworthy or unlovable, difficulty trusting anyone, and fear of getting close to people.

How This Affects Spiritual Life

These challenges go beyond just human relationships—they affect spiritual life as well. For example, people with a history of harsh or abusive parenting often find it difficult to see God as a loving, nurturing presence. Instead, they project the traits of their human caregivers onto God, viewing Him as distant, punitive or harsh and punishing, untrustworthy, and waiting to catch them doing something wrong. This spiritual disconnect can seriously hinder one's faith journey and contribute to feeling fragmented or broken inside.

The Gap in Christian Resources

Despite all the research on attachment theory, there's limited exploration of these issues from a Christian or Biblical perspective. Yet these findings align perfectly with what many people in Christian communities experience, highlighting a pressing need for targeted interventions.

If abusive or neglectful early experiences can distort how people relate to others and to God, then pastors, biblical counselors, and other Christian leaders must be equipped to address these complex issues. Resources and methods for addressing attachment-related challenges in a Christian context need to be developed. Ministry interventions that focus on reframing life narratives, changing how people see their stories, restoring trust, and reshaping internal models of self and God offer a pathway for healing. By fostering secure connections, both relational and spiritual, these interventions help people overcome the damaging effects of their early childhood experiences.

MEDIATORS: THE CATALYSTS FOR HEALING

Mediators play a crucial role in addressing disrupted attachment outcomes. Whether in the form of pastoral care, therapeutic relationships, or supportive faith communities, mediators act as bridges between past wounds and present healing.

Mediators facilitate the process of reframing one's understanding of relationships, both human and divine, by introducing new patterns of trust, intimacy, and positive interaction. This is particularly important for people who struggle with distorted images of God due to negative caregiver experiences. By creating environments of acceptance, compassion, and forgiveness, mediators help re-establish the relational foundation necessary for spiritual growth and emotional health. These efforts don't just help individuals, they also build stronger, healthier faith communities and churches.

INTERNAL WORKING MODELS: THE RELATIONSHIP BLUEPRINT

Attachment theory revolutionized the understanding of how early life experiences shape all relationships, including one's relationship with God. Bowlby and other researchers replaced the outdated idea that childhood permanently determines the future with a more hopeful view.

Instead, attachment theory emphasizes that early experiences influence how people relate to themselves, others, and God by forming what Bowlby called "internal working models." These are cognitive and emotional frameworks developed in childhood that guide how individuals perceive and respond to relationships throughout their lives.

Here's the encouraging news: these models are malleable or changeable. They can be transformed through reinterpretation, reconstruction, and intentional healing efforts.

What Are Internal Working Models?

Internal working models serve as blueprints for relationships. Think of them as mental templates that determine how people see themselves, how they view others, what they expect from relationships, and how they relate to God.

Positive early experiences lead to secure internal working models. Individuals view themselves as worthy of love, see others as trustworthy, and perceive God as benevolent, good and loving. Negative early experiences create insecure working models characterized by fear and mistrust, a distorted view of relationships, seeing oneself as unworthy, and viewing God as harsh or unreliable.

Research Support

McCarthy and Taylor examined the impact of abusive childhood experiences on adult relationships. Their research revealed that abusive childhoods often lead to dysfunctional romantic relationships in adulthood. These findings connect with theological perspectives, suggesting that people with negative internal working models will similarly struggle to form a secure and loving relationship with God as Father.

THE LONG SHADOW OF CHILDHOOD TRAUMA

Research consistently shows that abusive or neglectful parenting contributes to insecure attachment styles that can persist into adulthood. Bowlby argued that these attachment styles, developed in response to early caregiving behaviors, influence relational patterns throughout life, including one's perception of and connection to God.

Each attachment style affects views of God differently.

Avoidant Attachment

Individuals with avoidant attachment may view God as distant or irrelevant, mirroring the emotional unavailability of their caregivers. They might think God doesn't really care about them, so why bother with Him. They keep God at arm's length, just as they learned to do with people.

Resistant or Anxious Attachment

Those with resistant attachment might see God as inconsistent, oscillating between viewing Him as loving and punishing. This reflects the unpredictability of childhood relationships. They're never quite sure if God is pleased with them or angry at them.

Disorganized Attachment

People with disorganized attachment may perceive God as simultaneously comforting and threatening, embodying the duality of love and fear experienced in abusive caregiving contexts. They want to get close to God but are also terrified of Him. Their feelings about God are confusing and contradictory. Studies by Carranza and Kilmann, as well as Nicolosi, underscore these patterns. They demonstrate that childhood trauma, such as neglect or abuse, directly impacts adult romantic relationships and spiritual perceptions, often distorting understanding of love, trust, and authority.

CONSEQUENCES OF TRAUMA: RELATIONAL AND SPIRITUAL

Abusive parenting styles, marked by physical or emotional cruelty, disrupt a child's ability to form healthy relationships later in life. These consequences extend beyond human relationships to spiritual dimensions, influencing how individuals perceive and engage with God.

Distorted Perceptions of God

Many survivors of childhood trauma project the characteristics of their abusive caregivers onto their image of God. For example, if someone experienced harsh punishment as a child, they view God as punitive and unloving. If their parent was unpredictable, they see God as moody and unreliable. If their parent was emotionally absent, they perceive God as distant and uncaring.

Negative Self-Image

Childhood abuse often leads to feelings of unworthiness, poor self-esteem, and difficulty accepting love from others or God. Biblically, self-worth is rooted in being created and loved by God. But internalized messages of being "unlovable" or "bad" obstruct this understanding. Individuals might think that if their own parents couldn't love them, how could God, that they must be fundamentally flawed or broken, or that they don't deserve God's love.

Misinterpretation of Behavior

Research shows that survivors of childhood trauma are prone to misinterpreting the intentions of others, including God, as hurtful or harmful. This bias leads to a cycle of blame, thinking it's God's fault this bad thing happened, anger about why God would let this happen, and further alienation from meaningful relationships and spiritual connections. Even when God or others have good intentions, trauma survivors often perceive threat or harm.

WHAT THE EVIDENCE SHOWS: CASE STUDIES

Numerous case studies substantiate the profound effects of early trauma on relational and spiritual development. Children subjected to physical, emotional, or neglectful abuse often display heightened sensitivity to perceived rejection, seeing rejection even when it's not there. They show a tendency to expect pain or betrayal in close relationships, difficulty trusting others including God, and disengagement from faith practices such as church, prayer, and Bible reading.

These patterns continue into adulthood, as seen in McCarthy and Taylor's work. Their studies demonstrated that childhood trauma disrupts normal relational patterns and creates barriers to intimacy in both human and spiritual relationships.

THE THEOLOGICAL "PROBLEM:" GOD AS FATHER

Scripture presents God as a loving Father. But for many survivors of abuse, this image is loaded with pain and distrust. Biblical metaphors like "God is our Father," "The Bride of Christ," and "Children of God" offer profound relational connections, but trauma-based internal working models distort them. Survivors struggle to reconcile these divine representations with their lived experiences of punitive or neglectful caregivers.

Viewing God as Punitive

Survivors often equate God's discipline with punishment, reflecting their experiences of harsh caregiving. This perception fosters fear-based relationships with God, centered on avoidance, staying away from God so He won't hurt them, or appeasement, trying to be perfect so God won't punish them, rather than love and trust.

Rejecting God Out of Fear

Trauma can lead people to associate God with pain and suffering, reinforcing a belief that divine relationships are inherently harmful. These perceptions are often reinforced by negative religious experiences filtered through their trauma-based lens. For example, a harsh sermon about God's wrath confirms their fear, church discipline feels like abuse, or religious rules feel like the same controlling environment they grew up in.

HOW CHRISTIAN COUNSELING CAN HELP

The evidence makes it clear: counselors and faith leaders need to address the relational and spiritual wounds caused by childhood trauma. Christian counseling offers unique approaches to reframing these perceptions.

Reconstructing Internal Working Models

By identifying and challenging negative beliefs about caregivers and God, counselors help people develop healthier relational patterns. Techniques include cognitive reframing, changing how people think about past events, narrative therapy or rewriting one's life story, practicing forgiveness, and reinterpreting life stories in light of God's love and grace.

For example, instead of thinking "My father's abuse proves I'm worthless," individuals learn to think, "My father's abuse was about his brokenness, not my worth. God sees me as precious."

Promoting Healing Through Scripture

Biblical teachings about God's unconditional love, forgiveness, and faithfulness serve as powerful tools for healing. Helpful passages include Psalm 23, "The Lord is my shepherd," Matthew 11:28–30, "Come to me, all who are weary and burdened," Romans 8:38–39, "Nothing can separate us from God's love," and 1 John 4:18, "Perfect love casts out fear." These passages help survivors reimagine God as a source of comfort and rest rather than fear and punishment.

Fostering Community Support

Engaging in faith communities provides relational healing through shared experiences, showing people they're not alone, support networks with people who care, mentorship providing healthy models of what relationships should look like, and a sense of belonging. Healthy church communities help rebuild trust and show what unconditional love actually looks like in practice.

PRACTICAL STEPS FOR HEALING

For those dealing with trauma-based attachment issues, practical steps include several approaches. First, acknowledging the problem involves recognizing that early experiences have shaped how one sees God and relationships. Seeking help means finding a Christian counselor, pastor, or mentor who understands attachment theory and trauma. Challenging false beliefs involves stopping and countering thoughts like "God is just like my abusive father" with truth from Scripture. Engaging with community means joining a small group or church where healthy relationships can be experienced. Studying God's character involves reading the Bible specifically to learn about who God really is, not who trauma suggests He is. Being patient with oneself recognizes that healing takes time and deep patterns won't change overnight. Practicing vulnerability means starting small by opening up to safe people and to God in prayer.

CONCLUSION

The concept of internal working models offers valuable insight into how early attachment experiences shape relational and spiritual development. Trauma from abusive or neglectful parenting doesn't just disrupt human relationships—it also distorts one's view of God.

But here's the hopeful message: these challenges, while profound, are not insurmountable. Christian counseling, grounded in both psychological principles and theological truths, provides pathways to reframe the past, heal emotionally, and cultivate a secure and loving relationship with God.

By addressing the interplay between attachment and spirituality, counselors can guide individuals toward restoration, helping them embrace God's unconditional love, rebuild trust in divine and human relationships, develop healthy internal working models, and experience the freedom and peace God intended for them.

The past doesn't have to define the future. The damage from childhood trauma is real and significant, but it can be healed. Through mediators, whether counselors, pastors, mentors, or supportive faith communities, and through the ultimate Mediator, Jesus Christ, individuals can reconstruct their internal working models and develop a healthy, loving relationship with God and others.

People are not beyond help. They are not too broken. They are not unlovable. And with the right support and intentional effort, individuals can experience the fullness of relationship, both human and divine, that God designed them for.

CHAPTER 8: ATTACHMENT STYLES NEED MEDIATORS - JESUS FULFILLS THAT ROLE

The connection between psychology and spirituality provides a powerful way to understand how earliest relationships shape everything—not just how people connect with others, but also how they see and relate to God. Attachment styles, formed through early interactions with caregivers, create patterns that follow individuals throughout their lives. These patterns determine whether people can recognize and accept help from mediators.

At the heart of this chapter is a profound realization: unresolved trauma, especially childhood abuse or neglect, creates significant barriers to healthy relationships. This extends beyond just interpersonal relationships—it affects one's relationship with God, making it difficult to view Him as a loving, compassionate, and trustworthy Father.

Addressing these barriers requires understanding how attachment styles mediate or bridge between past trauma and present relational patterns, how these styles impact spiritual growth and self-esteem, and what steps are needed to heal and restore these foundational bonds. This chapter examines these challenges using both psychological research and biblical principles, highlighting the importance of overcoming barriers to establish secure and fulfilling relationships with others and with God.

HOW ATTACHMENT STYLES AFFECT SELF-ESTEEM

One of the most profound ways a perception of a punitive, harsh and punishing, or distant God affects individuals is in their self-esteem. From a biblical perspective, self-esteem is tied to one's soul and personal identity. When self-worth is damaged, often as a result of childhood trauma or abuse, it creates a significant barrier to forming close relationships, both with others and with God.

People who feel inherently "unlovable" struggle to accept the idea of a loving God who can heal and restore their wounds. If individuals believe they're fundamentally unworthy, why would God want a relationship with them? If they internalize the message that they're "bad" or "broken," how can they accept unconditional love?

Psychologist Erik Erikson's work on identity and relationships underscores the powerful influence of self-perception on one's ability to engage in healthy, intimate connections. If people internalize a belief that they're undeserving of love or care, it becomes increasingly difficult to accept God's unconditional love.

Biblically, this inability to embrace love reflects a lack of trust and acceptance that hinders spiritual growth, limits one's relationship with God as a loving Father, and keeps individuals stuck in patterns of shame and unworthiness.

ATTACHMENT STYLES AS MEDIATORS

Research by McCarthy and colleagues explores the concept of mediating factors - things that bridge early childhood experiences, particularly abusive ones, and future relational patterns. Their studies demonstrate that attachment styles—secure, avoidant, ambivalent, or disorganized—serve as descriptors of how trauma manifests in adult relationships. Attachment styles, particularly avoidant and ambivalent, often reflect the contradictory emotional behaviors rooted in unresolved early trauma.

What Research Shows

McCarthy and Taylor's work revealed a strong correlation between childhood abuse and dysfunctional relational patterns in adulthood. For instance, women who experienced abuse from a father or father figure often develop avoidant or ambivalent attachment styles.

These individuals long for emotional closeness but simultaneously create distance, reflect a deep-seated fear of being hurt or abandoned, and experience a push-pull dynamic in relationships. This push-pull pattern complicates their ability to form stable, loving relationships, perpetuating a cycle of insecurity and mistrust.

Consider someone who desperately wants a close relationship but sabotages it whenever things get too intimate. They might push their partner away when things feel "too good," create conflict to maintain emotional distance, test their partner constantly to see if they'll leave, and never fully trust that love is real or lasting. This isn't conscious behavior—it's a protective mechanism from trauma.

SPIRITUAL IMPLICATIONS OF ATTACHMENT STYLES

From a theological perspective, this attachment dynamic mirrors the internal conflict many people experience when trying to relate to God as Father. For those with a history of abuse, the desire for a loving relationship with God exists, but it's accompanied by an overwhelming fear of vulnerability and pain. This leads to a paradoxical pattern of drawing near to God and then withdrawing, which undermines the formation of a secure and trusting relationship.

Biblical Imagery That Can Feel Hollow

Biblical imagery such as God being a refuge as in Psalm 23, God as a shepherd, and God as protector can feel inaccessible or "ring hollow" to those whose early experiences taught them to associate authority figures with harm rather than protection. When an earthly father hurt someone, the idea of God as "Father" might trigger fear rather than comfort. The inability to reconcile these conflicting emotions creates an emotional and spiritual distance that can be very challenging to bridge.

HOW MEDIATION WORKS: THE RESEARCH

McCarthy and colleagues identified what they call "mediating factors." They observed a correlation between abusive childhood experiences and later dysfunction in loving relationships. They drew on principles set out by researchers Baron and Kenny in 1986.

The basic relationship works like this. Path A represents childhood abuse affecting attachment style. Path B shows attachment style affecting relationship quality. Path C represents the direct connection between childhood abuse and relationship quality.

The key insight is this: when researchers control for Paths A and B, meaning they account for attachment style as a mediator, the previously significant relationship between childhood abuse, the independent variable, and relationship quality, the outcome variable, is no longer significant.

In plain terms, this means that attachment style is the bridge between childhood abuse and adult relationship problems. If the attachment style, the mediator, can be changed, relationship quality can improve even though the childhood abuse that already happened cannot be changed.

According to McCarthy and colleagues, "From a theoretical perspective, when Path C is reduced to zero, this provides strong evidence for a single dominant mediator." This secular research demonstrates agreement with the Biblical perspective that mediators can transform outcomes.

FEARFUL AVOIDANT ATTACHMENT: THE ULTIMATE PARADOX

Attachment theory helps illuminate how early relational experiences shape interactions with others and perception of God. The "fearful avoidant" attachment style exemplifies the profound emotional challenges people face in seeking connection while simultaneously fearing it.

What Is Fearful Avoidant Attachment?

Fearful avoidant individuals live in a paradox of emotional longing and aversion. They desire closeness deeply but are terrified of the vulnerability and intimacy that relationships demand. They want connection but fear it at the same time, experiencing constant internal conflict.

This fear often stems from early life experiences such as childhood trauma, including emotional abuse, physical abuse, or sexual abuse, which disrupt the ability to form secure bonds. Growing up in alcoholic or abusive households, in unpredictable environments, fosters mistrust and emotional instability. Children never knew which version of their parent they would encounter.

In these contexts, relationships become fraught with contradiction and uncertainty. While the need for connection persists, the fear of rejection or emotional harm keeps people at a distance.

How This Affects Spiritual Life

This push-pull dynamic is especially pronounced in spiritual life. People with fearful avoidant attachment may yearn for intimacy with God but fear the emotional exposure it requires. They create a cycle of seeking and withdrawing, mirroring their human relationship patterns in their relationship with God.

For example, individuals feel drawn to pray but then avoid it because it feels too vulnerable. They want to trust God but are terrified He'll hurt or abandon them. They long for spiritual closeness but keep God at arm's length "just in case."

JESUS CHRIST: THE ULTIMATE MEDIATOR

For those struggling with fearful avoidant attachment, Jesus Christ offers a powerful avenue for healing. Within Biblical theology, Jesus is the ultimate Mediator, bridging the gap between humanity and God. This role is particularly significant for people whose attachment wounds hinder their ability to trust, connect, or feel secure in their relationship with God.

How Jesus Provides the Framework for Healing

Through His life, death, and resurrection, Jesus provides the power to form a framework for reconciliation and restoration.

Jesus embodies unconditional love and acceptance, qualities fearful avoidant individuals may have never experienced in their formative years. He offers a relationship without the threat of abandonment or harm, providing a safe pathway to God.

Jesus' sacrifice addresses not only sin but also deep emotional wounds through substitutionary atonement. He doesn't just forgive—He heals. He takes the punishment individuals feared, removing the barrier between them and God.

By understanding Christ's unchanging nature, people can begin to reframe their perceptions of love, trust, and connection. He is the same yesterday, today, and forever, as stated in Hebrews 13:8. Unlike human caregivers, He never changes, never abandons, never hurts. This provides a model of trust and security.

Why Jesus Is the Perfect Mediator for Fearful Avoidant Attachment

Jesus understands suffering, as described in Isaiah 53:3. He was rejected, so He understands rejection. He offers perfect love that casts out fear, according to 1 John 4:18. He provides the security fearful avoidant people desperately need but have never experienced.

SECULAR AND THEOLOGICAL CONVERGENCE

The concept of mediation resonates in both psychological and theological contexts, and they converge beautifully.

Psychological Mediation

Studies by researchers like Laura Carranza and Peter R. Kilmann highlight the importance of mediation in addressing the relational consequences of childhood trauma. These studies emphasize the role of therapeutic interventions in helping individuals process unresolved attachment issues, enabling them to form healthier adult relationships, and providing a safe relationship that models what healthy attachment looks like.

Spiritual Mediation

Christian theology positions Jesus as the ultimate Mediator who facilitates reconciliation and healing. He provides the way for individuals to transcend emotional barriers, experience the unconditional love of God, and reframe their identity and self-worth.

The Convergence Point

Both psychology and theology agree that mediation is essential for healing. Without a mediator, the direct path from trauma to dysfunction remains intact. With a mediator, transformation becomes possible.

The difference is that while human mediators such as therapists, counselors, and pastors can help people work through attachment issues, Jesus offers something more—a perfect, unchanging relationship that can heal even the deepest wounds.

PRACTICAL APPLICATION

For those who struggle with fearful avoidant attachment, several steps can facilitate healing.

Recognizing the pattern involves acknowledging that one has conflicting desires, wanting closeness while fearing it. Seeking human mediators means finding a therapist or Christian counselor who understands attachment theory and can help process trauma.

Engaging with Jesus as Mediator involves reading about His character in Scripture, noticing how He interacted with broken, hurting people, and practicing bringing fears and wounds to Him in prayer.

Starting small recognizes that complete trust doesn't have to happen right away. Taking small steps toward vulnerability and celebrating small victories builds momentum.

Finding a safe faith community means being part of a healthy church that can model what secure attachment looks like. Experiencing consistent, loving relationships helps rewire attachment patterns.

Being patient acknowledges that changing attachment patterns takes time. Individuals are rewiring deeply ingrained neural pathways. Healing is a journey, not a destination.

CONCLUSION

In the next chapter, the concept of mediation will be explored even deeper - both the secular understanding of a mediator's role and the theological perspective of Jesus as the ultimate Mediator. This exploration will underscore how Christ's unique position enables the restoration of fractured relationships, the healing of emotional wounds, and a secure, trusting relationship with "Our Father."

Several key understandings emerge from this chapter. Attachment styles serve as mediators between childhood trauma and adult relationship patterns. These patterns affect not just human relationships but one's relationship with God. Fearful avoidant attachment creates a push-pull dynamic that's especially challenging. Jesus Christ is the ultimate Mediator who can heal even the deepest attachment wounds. Both psychological research and Biblical theology point to the necessity and power of mediation. Healing is possible through both human mediators, such as therapists and counselors, and the divine Mediator, Jesus.

The message is clear: attachment style isn't one's identity—it's a pattern that can be changed. Through the right mediators, especially Jesus Christ, individuals can experience the secure, loving relationships they were designed for. The paradox of wanting closeness while fearing it can be resolved through the perfect love that casts out fear.

People don't have to live in that internal conflict forever. Healing is available. Connection is possible. And God is waiting with arms wide open, ready to be the Father individuals never had but always needed.

CHAPTER 9: JESUS THE CHRIST - THE ULTIMATE MEDIATOR

Throughout human history, relationships have been at the center of existence. Yet for many people, early childhood experiences marked by dysfunction or trauma distort their ability to form healthy, lasting bonds. John Bowlby's groundbreaking work on attachment theory demonstrated how early relationships, particularly with primary caregivers, shape the emotional and relational blueprint for life.

When these foundational relationships are marked by neglect, abuse, or inconsistency, they leave deep wounds that hinder both emotional and spiritual growth.

As discussed in previous chapters, research shows the need for a mediator to bridge the gap created by dysfunctional early attachments. Bowlby's studies and later research consistently demonstrate that the presence of a mediator, whether a supportive person or a structured intervention, can play a transformative role in repairing broken relational patterns.

This chapter explores the concept of a mediator, focusing on the unique and unparalleled role of Jesus Christ as the ultimate Mediator who not only reconciles human relationships but also restores the broken relationship between humanity and God.

THE MEDIATOR ROLE IN SECULAR PSYCHOLOGY

In secular psychology, the term "mediator" refers to a person or mechanism that intervenes to resolve or alleviate conflict. For people with insecure or dysfunctional attachment styles, mediators often take the form of therapists or counselors who use evidence-based techniques to address the lingering effects of childhood trauma.

How Secular Mediators Work

Studies like those by Alice Chornesky emphasize the critical role mediators play in helping repair attachment wounds. Chornesky's research reveals that therapeutic interventions can help individuals reframe their negative self-perceptions, develop healthier relational patterns, and improve their emotional resilience.

These mediators function by acknowledging the past, helping people confront and process the pain of their early experiences. Healing cannot occur without acknowledgment. They provide tools for healing, offering strategies for managing emotions, building trust, and forming secure relationships. They also encourage growth, guiding individuals toward greater emotional stability, relational satisfaction, and healthier patterns moving forward.

The Limitation of Secular Mediation

While these approaches can yield meaningful results, they're inherently limited. Secular mediators address the psychological and emotional dimensions of brokenness but struggle to resolve the spiritual disconnection that often underlies these issues.

A therapist can help individuals understand why they struggle to trust, provide tools to manage anxiety, and help develop better relationship patterns. However, a therapist cannot heal the deepest spiritual wounds, restore one's relationship with God, or give a new identity rooted in divine love.

This limitation highlights the necessity of a mediator who can address the whole person—spirit, soul encompassing mind, will, and emotions, and body.

THE MEDIATOR IN BIBLICAL THEOLOGY

In contrast to the secular perspective, the Bible presents a profoundly spiritual understanding of mediation. The biblical mediator is not merely an intermediary but a Divine agent of reconciliation and restoration. This role is fulfilled in its entirety by Jesus Christ.

Jesus serves as the bridge between humanity and God. Within that role, He is the ultimate Mediator for mankind.

JESUS: THE ONE AND ONLY MEDIATOR

The Bible clearly identifies Jesus Christ as the sole Mediator between God and humanity. First Timothy 2:5 states, "For there is one God and one mediator between God and mankind, the man Christ Jesus."

This verse emphasizes the exclusivity of Christ's role—He's the only one. It underscores the necessity of Christ's role—humanity needs Him. It speaks to the restoration of the broken relationship caused by sin.

Unlike human mediators who work to resolve interpersonal conflicts, Jesus mediates the eternal divide between sinful humanity and a holy God. This represents a far more profound mediation.

THE DEPTH OF CHRIST'S MEDIATION

Hebrews 9:15 demonstrates the depth of this mediation: "For this reason, Christ is the mediator of a new covenant, that those who are called may receive the promised eternal inheritance— now that he has died as a ransom to set them free from the sins committed under the first covenant."

Here, Christ's role as Mediator extends beyond mere reconciliation—it inaugurates a new covenant of mercy, grace, and redemption. Jesus pays the penalty for sin through His sacrificial death, liberates believers from condemnation, grants access to an eternal inheritance in God's kingdom, and creates a new relationship between God and humanity based on grace rather than law.

WHAT SETS JESUS APART: THREE AREAS OF HEALING

What sets Jesus apart as the ultimate Mediator is the all-encompassing nature of His work. His mediation addresses three critical areas of human brokenness.

Emotional Healing

For individuals carrying the scars of dysfunctional attachments, Jesus offers a safe haven of unconditional love. Unlike earthly relationships that may fail, His love is unwavering and healing. Psalm 147:3 declares, "He heals the brokenhearted and binds up their wounds."

Jesus invites individuals to bring their pain and suffering to Him, offering comfort and restoration. This isn't merely theoretical - it's a real, experienced healing that happens when people encounter His love.

Examples of emotional healing through Jesus include someone who felt abandoned by their father experiencing God's constant presence, someone who felt unworthy discovering they're deeply loved and valued, someone carrying shame finding complete acceptance and forgiveness, and someone filled with anxiety encountering the peace that passes understanding.

Relational Reconciliation

Jesus' mediation extends to human relationships, creating a life-altering pattern that enables people to forgive and seek forgiveness. Ephesians 4:32 instructs, "Be kind and compassionate to one another, forgiving each other, just as in Christ God forgave you."

Through His example and empowerment, Jesus equips believers to mend fractured relationships, build connections rooted in mercy and grace, extend to others the same forgiveness they've received, and break cycles of hurt and bitterness.

When individuals truly grasp how much God has forgiven them, it becomes easier to forgive others. When they experience unconditional love, they can extend that love to people who've hurt them.

Spiritual Renewal

The ultimate aim of Christ's mediation is spiritual renewal. By bridging the gap between humanity and God, Jesus restores believers to a position of righteousness and intimacy with the Father.

Romans 5:1-2 beautifully summarizes this truth: "Therefore, since we have been justified through faith, we have peace with God through our Lord Jesus Christ, through whom we have gained access by faith into this grace in which we now stand."

Spiritual renewal manifests as peace with God, no longer enemies but reconciled, access to God where individuals can approach Him freely, standing in grace representing a secure position not based on performance, and intimacy with the Father creating a personal relationship rather than distant religion.

JESUS AND ATTACHMENT HEALING

The profound impact of Jesus' mediation can be understood through the lens of attachment theory. Many people with insecure attachment styles struggle to trust others, fearing rejection or abandonment. This fear often extends to their relationship with God, making it difficult to fully embrace His love.

However, Jesus provides a secure attachment figure who is consistently loving. His love doesn't fluctuate based on performance or behavior. He is transcendent, and so is His love. Whether experiencing bad days or good days, His love remains constant. It cannot be earned, and it cannot be lost.

Jesus is perfectly reliable. His promises are absolutely sure. His presence is constant. He will never leave or forsake His followers, as stated in Hebrews 13:5. Unlike human caregivers who may have failed individuals, Jesus never will.

Jesus is unconditionally accepting. He welcomes all who come to Him, regardless of their past. No sin is too big, no wound too deep. People don't have to clean themselves up first. "Come as you are" isn't just a slogan—it's His invitation.

Reframing Through Jesus

By experiencing the steadfast love of Christ, individuals begin to reframe their understanding of relationships and develop a secure attachment to God as their heavenly Father.

The process unfolds as follows. People experience Jesus' unconditional love. This challenges their internal working models about relationships. They begin to see that not all authority figures will hurt them. They learn that love can be safe, consistent, and trustworthy. They develop a secure attachment to God. This secure attachment starts to overflow into their human relationships.

THEOLOGICAL SIGNIFICANCE

Christ's role as Mediator has profound theological significance. It affirms the necessity of divine intervention in human brokenness. It underscores the centrality of grace, demonstrating that people cannot earn their way to God. It shows that without Jesus, reconciliation with God would be impossible. It reveals that humanity would be trapped in a cycle of sin and separation without Him.

This isn't about religion or following rules - it's about relationship and rescue.

PRACTICAL IMPLICATIONS: HOW THIS CHANGES LIFE

On a practical level, embracing Jesus as Mediator can transform every aspect of life. It empowers individuals to face their past with confidence. Their identity is rooted in Christ, not in their experiences. What happened to them doesn't define them. Their worth comes from being loved by God, not from what others did or didn't do. They can look at their past without being controlled by it.

It enables people to build healthier relationships by modeling Christ's love and forgiveness in their interactions, breaking cycles of dysfunction, extending grace to others, and setting healthy boundaries while showing compassion.

It allows individuals to live with purpose, walking in the freedom and fullness of God's grace, experiencing life as God designed it, serving others from a place of security rather than insecurity, and making a difference because they're loved rather than to earn love.

WHAT THIS LOOKS LIKE IN REAL LIFE

Consider Sarah, who grew up with an abusive father and developed fearful avoidant attachment. Through encountering Jesus as her Mediator, she experienced unconditional love for the first time, learned that authority figures can be safe, developed a secure attachment to God as Father, was able to extend forgiveness to her earthly father, and built a healthy marriage instead of repeating patterns.

Marcus felt worthless because his parents were emotionally absent. Through Jesus as Mediator, he discovered his identity as a beloved child of God, found that his worth isn't based on performance, learned to accept love from others, and developed confidence and healthy relationships.

Elena saw God as harsh and punishing because that's how her caregivers were. Through Jesus as Mediator, she encountered God's grace and mercy, learned the difference between discipline and punishment, developed a loving relationship with God, and found freedom from fear-based religion.

COMPARING SECULAR AND SPIRITUAL MEDIATION

Secular mediation addresses psychological issues, provides helpful tools, and can improve emotional health. However, it cannot heal spiritual wounds, is limited to human wisdom and effort, and addresses symptoms but not root spiritual issues.

Spiritual mediation through Jesus addresses the whole person including spirit, soul, and body. It heals at the deepest level, provides not just tools but transformation, offers eternal rather than merely temporal solutions, works through divine power rather than just human effort, and addresses both symptoms and root causes.

The best approach combines both. Secular counseling and therapy can be incredibly helpful and represent a gift from God. However, they work best when combined with the spiritual healing Jesus offers. Individuals don't have to choose one or the other—they can use the tools God provides through both human wisdom and divine intervention.

CONCLUSION

Secular approaches to mediation, though valuable, fall short of addressing the spiritual dimensions of human brokenness. Only in Jesus Christ do people find a Mediator who heals holistically—emotionally, relationally, and spiritually.

His work transcends the limitations of human effort, offering a solution that is both eternal and transformative.

Several key understandings emerge. Human mediators such as therapists and counselors are valuable but limited. Jesus is the ultimate Mediator between God and humanity. His mediation addresses emotional, relational, and spiritual brokenness. He provides a secure attachment figure who is consistently loving, perfectly reliable, and unconditionally accepting. Through Him, individuals can reframe their internal working models and develop secure attachments. His mediation is exclusive—He's the only way to God—and necessary, as people can't accomplish this themselves. Experiencing Christ's love transforms not just one's relationship with God but all relationships.

The Invitation

As believers lean into the truth of Christ's mediation, they're invited to experience the fullness of God's love and the restoration of their most foundational relationship: the one with their Creator as Father.

Through Jesus, healing is not only possible but promised.

People don't have to carry the weight of broken attachments forever. They don't have to let their past define their future. They don't have to struggle alone with spiritual wounds that therapy alone can't heal.

Jesus stands ready as Mediator—ready to bridge the gap between brokenness and God's wholeness, between pain and His healing, between insecurity and His perfect love.

The question remains: Will individuals let Him? Will they bring their attachment wounds to the One who can heal them completely? Will they allow the ultimate Mediator to do what no human mediator can—restore them fully to relationship with their Heavenly Father?

He's waiting. His arms are open—He's extending His Hand. It's the Hand of the Father, and His love is unwavering.

CHAPTER 10: THE PERFECT MEDIATOR - PROPHET, PRIEST, AND KING

The biblical concept of a mediator is central to understanding God's plan for bringing humanity back to Himself. It reflects His deep desire to heal the brokenness caused by sin and restore relationships—both with Him and among His people. Throughout Scripture, humanity's need for someone to bridge the gap between a holy God and a sinful world becomes evident. This role is perfectly fulfilled in Jesus Christ.

This chapter explores the unique qualities that make Jesus the "perfect Mediator." Unlike human mediators, whose efforts may fix conflicts temporarily or superficially, Christ's mediation brings complete restoration, healing, and eternal reconciliation. His work as Mediator touches not only the brokenness of the present but also the wounds of the past, offering a comprehensive solution to the human condition.

Jesus' role as the perfect Mediator is foundational to Christian theology. By examining His divine nature, the depth of His sacrifice, and the fulfillment of His three roles—Prophet, Priest, and King—a deeper appreciation emerges of how He unites humanity with God. This union isn't merely about resolving conflicts or repairing fractured relationships; it's about bringing complete spiritual restoration, renewing hearts, and offering eternal hope.

WHY HUMANITY NEEDS A MEDIATOR

Since the fall of Adam and Eve in the Garden of Eden, humanity has been estranged from God. Sin doesn't just separate people from their Creator—it also distorts their relationships with God, others, and themselves. This separation manifests in various forms including guilt, shame, fear, and brokenness. All of these create barriers to spiritual and emotional healing.

Past traumas, painful childhood experiences, and unresolved emotional wounds make these barriers even worse. Many people struggle to form healthy attachments or find peace because the effects of sin and brokenness run deep.

The Secular Solution Falls Short

The secular world offers mediators—therapists, counselors, or negotiators—who aim to ease tensions and facilitate understanding. While these efforts are valuable, they often fall short of addressing the core spiritual needs that lie at the heart of human suffering.

The Biblical Solution

In contrast, the Bible presents Jesus as the ultimate answer. His work as Mediator addresses not only interpersonal conflicts but also the foundational problem of sin. Through Him, humanity is not merely reconciled to God—it is transformed and renewed. This transformative aspect of Christ's mediation sets Him apart as the perfect Mediator.

WHAT MAKES A BIBLICAL MEDIATOR DIFFERENT

The role of a Mediator in the Bible goes beyond the secular understanding of someone who intervenes between two opposing parties. A biblical mediator restores, reconciles, and unites. Jesus fulfills this role by creating a new covenant between God and humanity.

Hebrews 9:15 explains, "For this reason Christ is the Mediator of a new covenant, that those who are called may receive the promised eternal inheritance, now that He has died as a ransom to set them free from the sins committed under the first covenant."

This verse highlights the depth of Christ's mediatory work. His death wasn't just a symbolic act—it was a sacrificial offering that satisfied the demands of God's justice, extended God's mercy to sinners, and made eternal reconciliation possible.

The Old Covenant vs. The New Covenant

Under the old covenant, the relationship between God and His people was mediated through priests, sacrifices, and the Law.

These were temporary measures that pointed to the need for a greater mediator who could bring lasting reconciliation. Jesus, as the perfect Mediator, fulfilled the requirements of the law and established a new covenant based on grace.

His mediation isn't confined to religious rituals—it's deeply personal, offering individuals a direct and intimate relationship with God.

THE THREEFOLD ROLE OF JESUS AS MEDIATOR

Jesus' mediatory work can be understood through three roles He fulfills: Prophet, Priest, and King. These roles, each significant in their own right, come together in the person of Christ to make Him the perfect Mediator.

ROLE 1: JESUS AS PROPHET

What Was a Prophet in the Old Testament?

In the Old Testament, prophets were divinely chosen individuals who spoke on behalf of God. Their mission involved delivering messages of judgment, calling people to repentance, and revealing God's plans for the present and future.

Three key characteristics defined these prophets. First, they demonstrated integrity. Prophets were people of exceptional moral and spiritual integrity. They were set apart by their dedication to God and their commitment to living according to His will. Isaiah, upon seeing God's holiness, recognized his unworthiness, saying, "Woe is me, for I am undone! Because I am a man of unclean lips..." as recorded in Isaiah 6:5. Despite their imperfections, prophets were consecrated or set apart by God and empowered to deliver His messages.

Second, they served as messengers of God. Prophets served as God's spokespeople, delivering divine messages to His people. These messages often included warnings, promises, and calls for repentance. Jeremiah was tasked with warning Israel about coming judgment while offering hope for restoration. True prophets received direct revelations from God, which distinguished them from false prophets.

Third, they bore God's word. Prophets conveyed God's word with authority, offering guidance and hope. Amos 3:7 states, "Surely the sovereign Lord does nothing without revealing His plan to His servants, the prophets." These characteristics highlight the heavy responsibility of the prophetic office and foreshadow the ultimate Prophet—Jesus Christ.

Jesus' Identity as a Prophet

Jesus' prophetic identity is evident throughout the Gospels. In Matthew 13:57, Jesus acknowledges the rejection He faced in His hometown of Nazareth, saying, "A prophet is not without honor except in his hometown and his household." Here, He identifies Himself as a prophet, emphasizing the challenging nature of His mission.

In John 7:40–42, people debated whether Jesus was the prophet foretold in Deuteronomy 18:18, where God promised, "I will raise for them a prophet like you from among their brothers. I will put My words in His mouth, and He will tell them everything I command Him." This prophecy pointed to a prophet who would surpass all others—a role that Jesus uniquely fulfilled.

How Jesus Aligned with Old Testament Prophets

When examining Jesus' life and ministry, clear parallels emerge between Him and the Old Testament prophets. Just as prophets like Isaiah, Jeremiah, and Ezekiel received divine callings, Jesus' ministry began with a profound affirmation of His identity. At His baptism, the heavens opened, and the Spirit of God descended on Him like a dove, accompanied by a voice saying, "This is my Son, whom I love; with Him, I am well pleased," as recorded in Matthew 3:16-17. This event mirrors the divine callings of Old Testament prophets.

Like the prophets who conveyed God's messages, Jesus spoke with divine authority. John 12:49 records, "I did not speak on My own, but the Father who sent Me commanded Me to say all that I have spoken." His teachings weren't His own but were directly from the Father.

Prophets revealed God's plans and purposes, often through symbolic acts or visions. Jesus fulfilled this role perfectly, not only revealing God's will but embodying it. Luke 4:18 records His declaration: "The Spirit of the Lord is on me because He has anointed me to proclaim good news to the poor. He has sent me to proclaim freedom for the prisoners and recovery of sight for the blind." This declaration sums up His mission as the ultimate Prophet, bringing God's truth and salvation to humanity.

How Jesus Surpassed the Old Testament Prophets

While Jesus shares many characteristics with the Old Testament prophets, He also surpasses them in several ways. Unlike the Old Testament prophets who were fallible humans, Jesus lived a sinless life. His perfect integrity made Him the ultimate representative of God's holiness and truth.

Old Testament prophets often began their messages with "Thus says the Lord," indicating they spoke on God's behalf. Jesus, however, spoke with divine authority, often saying "I tell you," signifying His unity with the Father and His authority as God in the flesh.

While the prophets foretold the coming of the Messiah, Jesus was the fulfillment of those prophecies. His life, death, and resurrection completed the redemptive work foretold by the prophets, establishing Him as the ultimate Prophet who not only revealed God's plans but accomplished them.

The Rejection of Jesus as Prophet

Despite His wisdom, miracles, and divine authority, Jesus faced rejection, particularly from those who were familiar with Him. In Nazareth, people doubted His identity, asking, "Where did this man get this wisdom and these miraculous powers? Isn't this the carpenter's son?" as recorded in Matthew 13:54-55. Their familiarity with His earthly family blinded them to His divine mission, fulfilling the prophetic pattern of rejection seen in figures like Jeremiah and Isaiah.

This rejection underscores the challenge of recognizing God's work when it comes in unexpected forms. It also highlights the need for faith, as Jesus' miracles were often contingent on people's belief.

Jesus' Role as Prophet and Mediator

Jesus' role as Prophet is inseparable from His work as Mediator. As the ultimate Mediator, He not only conveyed God's words but also made reconciliation with God possible. Through His teachings, He revealed the Father's will. Through His sacrificial death, He bridged the gap between God and humanity.

The writer of Hebrews emphasizes this: "In the past, God spoke to our ancestors through the prophets at many times and in various ways, but in these last days, He has spoken to us by His Son," as stated in Hebrews 1:1-2. Jesus is not merely a prophet among many—He is the culmination of God's revelation and the embodiment of His redemptive plan.

ROLE 2: JESUS AS PRIEST

The concept of priesthood is central to understanding God's relationship with humanity. Priests served as intermediaries between God and His people, offering sacrifices, prayers, and intercessions on behalf of the community. Jesus Christ, the ultimate fulfillment of the priestly role, provides a transformative understanding of this function.

The Aaronic Priesthood: A Temporary System

The Aaronic priesthood, established under Aaron, Moses' brother, was integral to the Jewish covenant. This priesthood was characterized by strict duties, requirements, and rituals.

The responsibilities of the Aaronic priests included several key functions. First, offering sacrifices. Priests were responsible for offering sacrifices to atone for the sins of Israel. These sacrifices, which included animals and other offerings, symbolized repentance and obedience to God.

Second, ministry in the sanctuary. Priests represented the nation of Israel before God in the holy place. This ministry emphasized their role as intermediaries, standing in the gap between a holy God and sinful humanity.

Third, administering the law. Priests administered and interpreted the Law of Moses. They inquired of the Lord on behalf of Israel.

Fourth, annual atonement. On the Day of Atonement, Yom Kippur, the High Priest entered the Holy of Holies once a year to make atonement for the sins of the people, using the blood of sacrificial animals.

These duties reflected the reality of sin and the need for reconciliation between God and humanity. However, the Aaronic priesthood was inherently limited. It was temporary, tied to a specific lineage consisting of descendants of Levi and Aaron, and subject to human imperfection.

Strict Regulations

Priests had to meet stringent qualifications to serve. They had to marry only within their tribe. Physical blemishes disqualified individuals from priestly service. This emphasized the importance of holiness and perfection in representing God.

Yet despite their sacred duties, priests were allowed certain exemptions from the Law. For example, they worked on the Sabbath while offering sacrifices and declared lepers clean, acts that would otherwise render ordinary Israelites ceremonially unclean.

The Aaronic priesthood served as a shadow of something greater—a perfect and eternal priesthood that would be revealed in Jesus Christ.

The Priesthood of Melchizedek: A Unique and Eternal Order

The mysterious figure of Melchizedek appears briefly in Genesis 14:18-20, where he's described as both a king and a priest. Melchizedek's priesthood stands apart from the Aaronic priesthood in several key ways.

First, there was no lineage requirement. Unlike Aaronic priests, Melchizedek's priesthood wasn't based on ancestry or tribal affiliation. This signifies a universal and eternal priesthood.

Second, he united the roles of king and priest. Melchizedek united the roles of King and Priest, symbolizing authority and mediation. He blessed Abraham and received tithes from him, underscoring his spiritual status.

The New Testament identifies Jesus as a Priest in the order of Melchizedek, as stated in Hebrews 7:17. This comparison highlights the eternal and universal nature of Jesus' priesthood, which transcends the limitations of the Aaronic system.

Jesus as the High Priest

Jesus Christ fulfills and surpasses the roles of both the Aaronic priesthood and the priesthood of Melchizedek. As the ultimate High Priest, Jesus provides a complete and eternal solution to humanity's separation from God.

Fulfillment of the Aaronic Priesthood

Jesus fulfilled the requirements of the Aaronic priesthood by offering Himself as the ultimate sacrifice for sin. The key difference is clear: Aaronic priests offered repeated animal sacrifices that provided temporary atonement, while Jesus offered Himself once, providing eternal redemption.

Hebrews 9:12 states, "He entered the Most Holy Place once for all by His blood, thus obtaining eternal redemption." Additionally, Jesus serves in the heavenly sanctuary, the "true tabernacle" not made by human hands, as mentioned in Hebrews 8:2. This emphasizes His role as the eternal Mediator, bridging the gap between God and humanity in a way that the Aaronic priests could not.

Fulfillment of the Priesthood of Melchizedek

Jesus' priesthood reflects the characteristics of Melchizedek's order in three ways. First, its eternal nature. As a resurrected Savior, Jesus' priesthood is everlasting. He continues to intercede for humanity at the right hand of God.

Second, its universal significance. Jesus' priesthood extends to all nations, uniting Jews and Gentiles in one covenant.

Third, the perfect sacrifice. While Melchizedek received tithes and gave blessings, Jesus offered Himself, demonstrating the ultimate act of priestly mediation.

Jesus' High Priestly Ministry

Jesus exhibited His high priestly role in several ways. First, intercession for humanity. Jesus' ministry as High Priest includes ongoing intercession. Before His crucifixion, He prayed for His disciples and all future believers in His High Priestly Prayer recorded in John 17. He asked the Father to protect His followers, sanctify them or make them holy, and unify them. This prayer reflects Jesus' deep concern for humanity and His mediating role between God and His people.

Second, entering the holiest of all. In the Old Testament, the High Priest entered the Holy of Holies once a year to make atonement with the blood of animals. Jesus, however, entered the heavenly Holy of Holies with His own blood, securing eternal redemption for all who believe in Him. This act signifies the ultimate fulfillment of the priestly role.

Third, bridging the gap. As both fully human and fully divine, Jesus uniquely bridges the gap between God and humanity. He understands human struggles and weaknesses because He is fully human. He embodies divine perfection because He is fully God. This dual nature makes Him the perfect Mediator.

ROLE 3: JESUS AS KING

The kingship of Jesus is a central theme in Christianity, vividly portrayed throughout the Gospels and affirmed by His words and actions. His identity as King was not only a cornerstone of His earthly ministry but also a revelation of His divine mission to establish an eternal kingdom. Jesus' kingship transcends earthly paradigms, uniting spiritual and temporal realms under His sovereign rule.

Jesus Knew He Was King

Jesus was fully aware of His identity as King throughout His time on earth. He spoke about His kingdom more than 100 times in the Gospels. His teachings and parables frequently revolved around the "Kingdom of God" or the "Kingdom of Heaven." For example, Jesus began His ministry by declaring, "Repent, for the kingdom of heaven has come near," as recorded in Matthew 4:17.

Jesus Before Pilate

One of the most profound affirmations of Jesus' kingship came during His trial before Pontius Pilate. When Pilate questioned Him about being the King of the Jews, Jesus responded, "My kingdom is not of this world. If it were, my servants would fight to prevent my arrest by the Jewish leaders. But now my kingdom is from another place," as stated in John 18:36.

Pilate pressed further, asking, "You are a king, then!" To this, Jesus replied, "You are right in saying I am a king. In fact, for this reason, I was born and came into the world—to testify to the truth," according to John 18:37.

Here, Jesus clarified the nature of His kingship. It's not rooted in earthly power or political systems. It's based on divine authority and eternal truth. His kingdom represents a spiritual realm that transcends human constructs. It offers eternal hope and salvation to all who believe.

The Nature of Jesus' Kingship

Unlike earthly kings, who derive their authority from ancestry, conquest, or law, Jesus' kingship is uniquely divine and eternal. First, His royal lineage. His royal lineage traces back to King David, fulfilling Old Testament prophecies. Isaiah 9:6-7 proclaims the coming of a ruler who will establish an everlasting kingdom of peace and righteousness.

Second, the priest-king order. Jesus' kingship aligns with the order of Melchizedek, the priest-king mentioned in Genesis and Psalm 110. The writer of Hebrews underscores this connection, describing Jesus as a king whose reign is eternal and unbounded by human limitations. Under the Mosaic Law, the roles of priest and king were strictly separate. Yet Jesus united these roles in Himself. As both High Priest and King, He mediates between God and humanity and reigns with justice and grace.

Third, the universal kingdom. Jesus' kingship is not confined to Israel but extends to all nations. His kingdom is inclusive, inviting people from every tribe, tongue, and nation to partake in its blessings. This universality is evident in Jesus' Great Commission: "Go and make disciples of all nations," as stated in Matthew 28:19.

Fourth, the spiritual kingdom. The spiritual nature of Jesus' kingdom distinguishes it from earthly ones. It is characterized by righteousness, peace, and joy in the Holy Spirit, as mentioned in Romans 14:17. Unlike temporal kingdoms, which rise and fall, His reign is eternal. Revelation 11:15 proclaims, "The kingdom of the world has become the kingdom of our Lord and His Messiah, and He will reign forever and ever."

Jesus' Kingship Brings Restoration

Jesus' kingship also brings restoration to broken relationships. Many people struggle to relate to God as a loving Father due to imperfect relationships with earthly fathers or negative experiences with authority figures. These struggles can lead to a sense of disconnection—what has been termed spiritual attachment disorder.

As King, Jesus offers healing and restoration. His reign is marked by compassion and understanding, providing a safe and nurturing relationship for those who feel distant from God. He invites all to come to Him, saying, "Come to me, all you who are weary and burdened, and I will give you rest," as recorded in Matthew 11:28.

Truth and Justice

Jesus' kingship is rooted in truth and justice, distinguishing Him from earthly rulers who are often swayed by corruption or personal ambition. During His trial, He declared, "For this reason, I was born and came into the world: to testify to the truth," according to John 18:37.

His kingdom is built on the unshakable foundation of God's truth, offering stability and security to His followers. As King, Jesus also upholds perfect justice. He will one day judge the living and the dead, as described in Matthew 25:31–46. In this final judgment, Jesus will separate the righteous from the unrighteous, reward those who have proclaimed Him both Lord and Savior, enable them to walk in grace and mercy, live according to His teachings, and overcome their past hurts.

The Vision in Revelation

The Book of Revelation provides a vivid picture of Jesus' kingship in its full glory. John describes Him as "the faithful witness, the firstborn from the dead, and the ruler of the kings of the earth," as stated in Revelation 1:5. Jesus is depicted as the Lamb who was slain, now exalted and reigning over all creation. Revelation 19:16 proclaims His title: "King of kings and Lord of lords." This vision of Jesus as King assures believers that His reign is supreme and unassailable. Despite the trials and tribulations of the present age, His kingdom will ultimately triumph.

Revelation 21:3-4 paints a picture of this glorious future, where God's people will dwell with Him in a renewed creation, free from pain, sorrow, and death.

Living Under the Reign of King Jesus

As followers of Jesus, believers are called to live as citizens of His kingdom. This involves several commitments.

First, declaring Jesus as Lord and Savior, proclaiming His suffering, death, and resurrection as atonement for sin. Second, aligning with His teachings by living according to His values and principles. Third, embodying kingdom principles of love, humility, and service. Jesus demonstrated these qualities during His earthly ministry—washing His disciples' feet and laying down His life for humanity.

Fourth, participating in His mission by being ambassadors of Christ, sharing the Gospel and working for justice, peace, and reconciliation in the world. This mission reflects the prayer Jesus taught His disciples: "Your kingdom come, Your will be done, on earth as it is in heaven," from Matthew 6:10.

The Hope of His Return

The kingship of Jesus provides believers with the hope of His return, when He will establish His kingdom in its fullness. This hope sustains Christians in times of difficulty, reminding them that their struggles are temporary and a glorious future awaits. Paul writes in Philippians 3:20-21, "Our citizenship is in heaven. And we eagerly await a Savior from there, the Lord Jesus Christ, who... will transform our lowly bodies so that they will be like His glorious body."

Until that day, believers are called to remain faithful, trusting in the sovereignty of King Jesus and looking forward to the day when "the earth will be filled with the knowledge of the glory of the Lord as the waters cover the sea," as prophesied in Habakkuk 2:14.

CONCLUSION: THE PERFECT MEDIATOR

Through His roles as Prophet, Priest, and King, Jesus serves as the ultimate Mediator between God and humanity. The Apostle Paul emphasizes this in 1 Timothy 2:5: "For there is one God and one Mediator between God and men, the man Christ Jesus."

This mediatorial role is also highlighted in Hebrews 8:6, which describes Jesus' ministry as superior to the old covenant because it is based on better promises, sealed by His sacrificial blood.

As the perfect Mediator, Jesus bridges the gap caused by sin, reconciles humanity to the Father, and ensures that His mediation is not only effective but also eternal. Through His death and resurrection, Jesus established a New Covenant, granting believers direct access to the Father and the promise of eternal life.

WHY JESUS IS THE PERFECT MEDIATOR

What makes Jesus the perfect Mediator can be summarized through His three roles.

As Prophet, He reveals God's truth perfectly, embodies God's word completely, surpasses all previous prophets, and serves as the final and complete revelation of God.

As Priest, He offers the perfect sacrifice, Himself, provides eternal atonement, intercedes for humanity continually, and bridges the gap between God and humanity.

As King, He reigns with perfect justice and truth, offers restoration to broken relationships, provides eternal security, and will return to establish His kingdom fully.

Together, these three roles make Jesus uniquely qualified to be the perfect Mediator. No human mediator—no therapist, counselor, or spiritual leader—can offer what Jesus offers: complete healing encompassing emotional, relational, and spiritual dimensions, eternal reconciliation with God, transformation from the inside out, and hope for both this life and the next.

The truth is simple but profound: Jesus is not just a mediator—He is the Mediator. The perfect one. The only one who can truly heal the deepest wounds of the soul and restore one's relationship with God.

For those struggling with attachment wounds, spiritual disconnection, or broken relationships, Jesus stands ready as the perfect Mediator. He understands human pain because He is fully human. He has the power to heal because He is fully divine. He has already done the work through His death and resurrection.

The question remains: Will individuals accept His mediation? Will they let the perfect Prophet reveal God's truth to them? Will they let the perfect Priest intercede for them? Will they let the perfect King reign in their lives?

He's waiting. And His mediation is perfect, complete, and eternal.

CHAPTER 11: SPIRITUAL ATTACHMENT DISORDER - WHEN CONNECTION WITH THE FATHER SEEMS IMPOSSIBLE

Spiritual Attachment Disorder occurs when individuals have serious difficulty seeing God as a loving, trustworthy figure or experiencing a meaningful spiritual relationship with Him. These struggles often stem from early-life experiences, particularly how "father" caregivers or authority figures treated them.

Such experiences create internalized "working models" - mental blueprints that influence how people view themselves, others, and their relationship with God the Father.

This chapter explores the roots of Spiritual Attachment Disorder, or SAD, how it manifests in spiritual life, the profound impact it can have on one's faith journey, and what can be done about it. Drawing on attachment theory and research by notable psychologists, the discussion examines how early relationships shape spiritual attachment and addresses ways to foster healing and restoration.

THE FOUNDATION: ATTACHMENT THEORY REFRESHER

Attachment theory from the earlier chapters provides the foundation for understanding Spiritual Attachment Disorder. Attachment theory, developed by John Bowlby and further refined by Mary Ainsworth, helps illuminate how early relationships influence emotional and relational development. Bowlby's key insight reveals that children are born with an inherent need to form bonds with caregivers. These bonds are essential for survival, emotional stability, and learning how relationships work. Through consistent caregiving, children develop internal working models—mental frameworks that define their expectations of relationships. These models shape their sense of self-worth, their capacity to trust others, and their ability to seek comfort during times of distress.

The Three Primary Attachment Styles

Secure attachment is marked by trust, comfort, and confidence in relationships. Individuals with secure attachment believe people will be there for them and feel worthy of love.

Insecure-avoidant attachment is characterized by emotional detachment and difficulty depending on others. Those with avoidant attachment keep people at arm's length to avoid being hurt.

Insecure-anxious attachment is defined by fear of abandonment, excessive neediness, and uncertainty in relationships. Individuals with anxious attachment constantly worry people will leave them.

Mary Ainsworth's Strange Situation Experiment, discussed in Chapter 1, demonstrated how these styles manifest in childhood and persist into adulthood unless addressed.

Later researchers, such as Nicolosi in 1991 and 2016, extended attachment theory to explore its implications in various life domains, including spirituality. They observed that just as early attachments influence human relationships, they also shape how individuals perceive and relate to God. This is where Spiritual Attachment Disorder enters the discussion.

THE ROOTS OF SPIRITUAL ATTACHMENT DISORDER

Spiritual Attachment Disorder emerges when disruptions in early attachments distort one's perception of God and spirituality. The ability to form a healthy spiritual connection is intricately linked to the attachment style developed during childhood.

How Caregivers Shape Views of God

Caregivers serve as a child's first experience of authority, protection, and unconditional love. When caregivers provide consistent care, love, and support, children are more likely to view God as a loving and dependable figure.

However, when caregiving is inconsistent, neglectful, or abusive, children internalize a distorted view of authority figures—and they carry that view into their relationship with God.

Examples of How This Works

When children experience rejection from caregivers, they might struggle to trust in God's love, fearing rejection in their spiritual relationship. They think, "If my own parents didn't want me, why would God?" or "I must be fundamentally unlovable."

When children are subjected to harsh discipline, they might perceive God as punitive or unapproachable, thinking "God is just waiting for me to mess up so He can punish me" or "I can never be good enough for God."

When children are emotionally neglected, they may find it challenging to seek comfort in God, feeling unworthy of divine care. They believe "God doesn't care about my problems; they're too small" or "I shouldn't bother God with my needs."

These early experiences create "spiritual working models" mental blueprints that shape how individuals approach prayer, worship, their faith, their faith community, and the Divine as Father.

The Persistence of Working Models

According to Bowlby, working models are persistent mental frameworks that influence how people interact with others and interpret the world. When these models are disrupted during childhood, they often carry over into adulthood, affecting relationships, parenting styles, and spiritual life.

For instance, individuals with insecure attachment styles may feel unworthy of God's love, questioning their place in His kingdom. They struggle to experience intimacy in prayer, fearing vulnerability. They harbor resentment toward God, particularly if they equate Him with past abusive or neglectful caregivers.

Without intervention, these patterns can lead to a cycle of spiritual alienation, emotional distress, and perpetuating feelings of loneliness and disconnection.

HOW SPIRITUAL ATTACHMENT DISORDER SHOWS UP

Spiritual Attachment Disorder can manifest in various ways, often reflecting one's underlying attachment style. Three main manifestations emerge.

Manifestation 1: Avoidant Attachment to Spirituality

Individuals with avoidant attachment approach spirituality with emotional detachment, reflecting their difficulty in forming close bonds. They perceive God as distant or uninvolved, mirroring their tendency to avoid vulnerability in human relationships. They show reluctance to engage in personal prayer or intimate forms of worship, as these activities require openness and trust, which feel dangerous.

Religious practices become transactional. People go through the motions, feeling like mere obligations, devoid of heartfelt connection or spiritual intimacy. The attitude becomes "I'll do what's required, but I won't let myself get emotionally involved." Consider Mark, who attends church every Sunday, participates in small group discussions, and even serves on a committee. But he never prays deeply, never shares his real struggles, and keeps God at arm's length emotionally. His faith is all head knowledge, no heart connection.

Manifestation 2: Anxious Attachment to Spirituality

Those with anxious attachment experience a heightened fear of losing God's favor, leading to overwhelming insecurity in their spiritual lives. They live with a constant fear of losing God's approval and engage in excessive religious rituals, seeking constant reassurance of God's love and acceptance. Despite their efforts, feelings of guilt and unworthiness dominate their spiritual experiences, creating a cycle of striving for divine approval and self-condemnation.

This leaves them spiritually exhausted, as their relationship with God becomes marked by fear rather than trust.

Consider Sarah, who prays multiple times a day, confessing the same sins over and over because she's never sure God has really forgiven her. She constantly worries she's not doing enough for God. She reads the Bible obsessively, looking for reassurance that God still loves her. Every minor mistake sends her into spiritual panic: "Did I just lose my salvation?"

Manifestation 3: Disorganized Attachment to Spirituality

For individuals with a history of trauma, disorganized attachment leads to deeply conflicted spiritual experiences. They simultaneously seek and fear God's presence, reflecting the unpredictable and chaotic nature of early relationships with caregivers. Trusting in God's goodness becomes a significant challenge as internalized working models portray authority figures as unreliable or harmful.

This inner conflict often results in persistent spiritual struggles, ongoing doubt, and difficulty experiencing peace or assurance in faith.

Consider David, who desperately wants a relationship with God but feels terrified whenever he tries to pray. He'll draw close to God for a while, then suddenly pull away in fear. He can't reconcile the idea of a loving God with his experiences of abuse from his father, who was a church leader. He wants to trust God but simultaneously expects God to hurt him.

THE BROADER IMPACT OF SPIRITUAL ATTACHMENT DISORDER

The consequences of Spiritual Attachment Disorder extend far beyond personal faith. It significantly influences various aspects of life, including emotional well-being, interpersonal relationships, and community engagement.

Impact on Human Relationships

Individuals struggling with SAD often have difficulty with intimacy, trust, and vulnerability in all relationships, which mirrors the challenges they face in their connection with God.

Someone with avoidant spiritual attachment may also avoid closeness with loved ones, fearing emotional dependence or rejection. Those with anxious attachment styles may exhibit clinginess, excessive reassurance-seeking, or fear of abandonment in their relationships. Disorganized attachment creates instability, oscillating between seeking connection and pushing others away.

This creates strained relationships with partners, family members, and friends. SAD thus not only affects spiritual life but also undermines the capacity to form healthy and meaningful bonds with others.

Impact on Emotional Well-Being

SAD significantly influences emotional well-being, often manifesting in persistent feelings of guilt, shame, and unworthiness. These emotions arise from a distorted perception of God as punitive, distant, and unapproachable. This creates a sense of spiritual inadequacy.

For individuals with anxious attachment, excessive self-criticism, fear of Divine rejection, and chronic anxiety develop. Over time, these can escalate to depression or hopelessness.

For individuals with disorganized attachment, profound inner conflict and spiritual turmoil emerge. The simultaneous desire for and fear of closeness with God creates confusion and feelings of being spiritually "stuck." This amplifies feelings of despair and frustration.

Impact on Faith Community Participation

Difficulty connecting with God often translates into challenges engaging with communal worship, service, or fellowship.

For individuals with avoidant attachment, involvement in faith-based activities feels superficial or obligatory, lacking genuine connection or joy. They're just going through the motions.

For individuals with anxious attachment, overcommitting to religious activities to gain acceptance or reassurance potentially leads to burnout or disillusionment. They never feel like they're doing enough.

For individuals with disorganized attachment, feelings of mistrust and fear of rejection deter meaningful connections within their faith community. Social isolation results, and they miss out on the support and encouragement communities typically provide.

HEALING S A D

Here's the encouraging news: Healing from Spiritual Attachment Disorder is possible. It requires intentional effort and often involves both psychological and spiritual interventions.

Step 1: Acknowledge the Foundation

The healing process starts with acknowledging Jesus as both Lord and Savior, allowing the Holy Spirit to shine His light on the influences of early attachments, identifying patterns and triggers, and beginning to reframe perceptions of God and authority figures.

Step 2: Understand Jesus as Mediator

Understanding the role of Jesus Christ as Mediator becomes pivotal, as discussed in Chapters 8 through 10. Jesus' role as the perfect Mediator offers hope for those struggling with spiritual attachment.

Romans 8:38-39 affirms that nothing can separate believers from God's love: "For I am convinced that neither death nor life, neither angels nor demons, neither the present nor the future, nor any powers, neither height nor depth, nor anything else in all creation, will be able to separate us from the love of God that is in Christ Jesus our Lord."

Jesus' earthly ministry exemplifies God's compassionate nature, providing a model of trustworthiness and accessibility. His invitation, "Come to me, all you who are weary and burdened, and I will give you rest," from Matthew 11:28, resonates deeply with those yearning for a secure spiritual connection.

Step 3: Consider Professional Help

For some, psychological support is an essential part of addressing SAD. Attachment-focused therapy, led by professionals trained in attachment theory, can help individuals explore relational patterns and working models, develop self-awareness, and reframe distorted beliefs about God, self, and others.

Individuals should look for a therapist with training in attachment theory, a Christian counselor who integrates faith and psychology, and someone who understands trauma and its spiritual implications.

Step 4: Engage in Inner Healing Prayer

Inner healing prayer is a Christ-centered practice that can be transformative. This approach involves inviting God into past wounds, allowing Jesus' shed blood to bring emotional and spiritual restoration, addressing underlying hurts, and beginning to experience healing and renewed connection with God as Father.

The process works by praying through specific painful memories, (and yes – we do have them) asking Jesus to reveal His presence in those moments, allowing the Holy Spirit to bring truth and healing, and replacing lies with God's healing truths.

Step 5: Join a Supportive Faith Community

Engaging with a supportive faith community—a local Bible-based church—is another valuable intervention. Benefits include being part of a group that reinforces positive spiritual connections, fostering a sense of belonging and accountability, instrumental reinforcement of spiritual growth and healing, and experiencing healthy relationships that model secure attachment.

Individuals should look for a church that emphasizes God's grace, not just rules, small groups where vulnerability is possible, mentorship opportunities, and a community that accepts imperfect people.

PRACTICAL PRACTICES FOR SPIRITUAL GROWTH

In addition to the interventions above, specific practices can nurture spiritual growth and aid in the healing process.

Practice 1: Journaling

Journaling provides a structured way to reflect on Scripture and personal experiences. Benefits include helping process emotions, recognizing patterns, deepening relationship with God, and tracking spiritual growth over time.

The practice involves setting aside ten to fifteen minutes daily, writing about what one is learning in Scripture, recording prayers and God's answers, and reflecting on how one is seeing God differently.

Practice 2: Intentional Prayer

Intentional prayer is a powerful tool for fostering intimacy with God. These practices focus on encouraging trust and vulnerability, quiet reflection and surrender, and cultivating deeper awareness of God's presence and love through His Holy Spirit.

Types to try include contemplative prayer, sitting in silence with God, prayer journaling, praying Scripture back to God, and listening prayer, waiting for God to speak.

Practice 3: Mentorship

Trusted spiritual mentors can offer guidance, encouragement, and accountability. They walk alongside individuals as they work to rebuild their faith. Benefits include a mentor's insight and experience helping navigate challenges, providing steady support and wisdom, modeling healthy spiritual attachment, and offering perspective when one feels stuck.

Individuals should look for someone with mature faith, good listening skills, personal experience with healing and growth, and wisdom and discernment.

Step 6: Be Patient with the Process

Addressing Spiritual Attachment Disorder is a journey that requires intentionality, patience, and faith. Important reminders include that healing doesn't happen overnight, setbacks are normal, progress isn't always linear, and God is patient with individuals in this process.

REAL-LIFE TRANSFORMATION STORIES

Example 1: From Avoidant to Secure

Tom grew up with an emotionally distant father and developed avoidant attachment. For years, his faith was intellectual only—no emotional connection. Through therapy, inner healing prayer, and a men's small group, he gradually learned to open up emotionally to God, experience God's presence in prayer, trust that vulnerability with God is safe, and develop a warm, personal relationship with his Heavenly Father.

Example 2: From Anxious to Secure

Lisa's childhood was marked by unpredictable parenting, leading to anxious attachment. Her spiritual life was exhausting—constantly striving, never feeling good enough.

Through understanding grace versus works, attachment-focused therapy, journaling God's promises, and a supportive church community, she learned to rest in God's unconditional love, trust that her salvation is secure, approach God with confidence rather than fear, and experience peace in her faith.

Example 3: From Disorganized to Secure

Carlos experienced severe abuse from his father, a religious leader, creating disorganized attachment. He simultaneously longed for and feared God. Through trauma-focused therapy, inner healing prayer, patient mentorship, and slowly experiencing healthy Christian community, he began to separate his father's actions from God's character, trust that God would not harm him, experience God's love without fear, and find stability and peace in his faith.

CONCLUSION: HOPE FOR HEALING

Spiritual Attachment Disorder is not a permanent condition. With intentional effort and divine grace, individuals can experience profound healing and restoration.

Rebuilding a secure spiritual attachment involves recognizing God's unchanging love, reframing distorted beliefs, embracing practices that nurture intimacy with Him, and allowing Jesus to mediate between one's brokenness and God's wholeness.

The Key Truth

Early experiences shaped views of God, but they don't have to define one's relationship with Him forever. God is not like caregivers who failed. He is perfectly loving, completely trustworthy, always available, never changing, and infinitely patient with the healing process.

The Journey Toward Wholeness

The journey toward spiritual wholeness is deeply personal yet universally accessible. It's an invitation to encounter God not as a distant authority figure but as a loving Father, recognizing Jesus as a compassionate Savior and faithful companion.

Several truths bear remembering. People are not too broken for God to heal. Attachment wounds don't disqualify anyone from His love. Healing is possible, no matter how deep the wounds. God specializes in restoration.

For those who struggle with Spiritual Attachment Disorder, several affirmations stand: they're not alone, it's not their fault, help is available, healing is possible, and God is waiting with open arms.

The invitation stands: "Come to me, all you who are weary and burdened, and I will give you rest," from Matthew 11:28.

The questions remain: Will individuals accept it? Will they let God be the Father they never had but always needed? Will they allow Jesus to mediate between their broken view of God and the reality of who He truly is?

The journey may be long, but it's worth it. And people don't have to walk it alone. God Himself walks with them, the Holy Spirit guides them, and Jesus intercedes for them.

Spiritual healing can start now.

CHAPTER 12: FOUR ATTACHMENT TYPES – THE IMPORTANCE OF THE ROLE OF THE FATHER

Attachment theory, developed by John Bowlby and expanded by Mary Ainsworth, provides a comprehensive framework for understanding how early relationships profoundly influence emotional and social development throughout the lifespan. While the theory initially focused on how infants form bonds with their primary caregivers and how these early experiences shape their capacity to form relationships later in life, the field has evolved significantly. Contemporary psychologists now explore how attachment styles continue to influence people throughout adulthood, particularly in intimate relationships, social dynamics, and—as this chapter will demonstrate—in one's relationship with God.

Building on Ainsworth's foundational work, researchers Hazan and Shaver, later expanded by Bartholomew and Horowitz, identified four primary attachment archetypes that offer a comprehensive view of emotional patterns, relationship behaviors, and the ways people interact with others based on their early experiences. These four attachment styles—Secure, Preoccupied (Anxious/Ambivalent), Fearful, and Dismissive (Avoidant)—can be understood through two fundamental axes: how individuals view themselves (positive versus negative) and how they view others (positive versus negative). This creates four distinct quadrants, each representing a unique pattern of relating to others and, significantly, to God.

Understanding these attachment styles offers valuable insight into how individuals approach relationships and can guide personal growth, healing, and the development of healthier connections. More importantly for the purposes of spiritual formation, these patterns reveal how early relational experiences shape one's capacity to trust, experience intimacy, and ultimately rest in the loving care of a Heavenly Father.

The Four Attachment Archetypes

Secure Attachment: The Foundation of Trust

Individuals with secure attachment generally possess a strong sense of self-worth and feel confident in their relationships, representing the intersection of a positive view of self and a positive view of others. These individuals are comfortable with both intimacy and independence, meaning they can enjoy closeness without feeling smothered or overly dependent. They believe they are lovable and expect others to see them the same way, anticipating acceptance and understanding from those around them. This fundamental trust makes them confident and balanced in both personal and social connections.

In relationships, securely attached individuals can be close without losing themselves and can be independent without feeling lonely. Trust comes naturally to them, and they communicate openly and honestly, creating reciprocal and emotionally healthy connections. Consider Emma, who grew up with loving, consistent parents. In her romantic relationship, she feels secure, she can be vulnerable without fear, gives her partner space without anxiety, and communicates her needs clearly. The foundation her parents provided has equipped her to navigate adult relationships with confidence and grace.

Spiritually, it is remarkably easy for secure individuals to rest in God's protection and love and relate to Him as a child would to a loving father. They trust God's goodness, feel comfortable approaching Him, do not struggle with feelings of unworthiness or distance, and experience intimacy in prayer naturally. Emma talks to God like a trusted friend and father, sharing her joys and struggles freely. Her secure attachment provides a relational template that translates seamlessly into spiritual intimacy, allowing her to receive God's love without the barriers that plague those with insecure attachment patterns.

Preoccupied Attachment: The Hunger for Reassurance

People with preoccupied attachment, characterized by a negative view of self-combined with a positive view of others, often struggle with feelings of unworthiness or inadequacy. While they maintain a positive view of others, they are deeply conscious of their own perceived flaws and harbor intense fears of abandonment. This creates a relational dynamic in which they focus excessively on their relationships, seeking constant reassurance and validation from loved ones. They may appear clingy or overly demanding as they attempt to compensate for their insecurities by seeking attention and support.

In relationships, these individuals need constant reassurance, asking repeatedly whether they are still loved—and fear abandonment intensely. They may become anxious when their partner is unavailable and often sacrifice their own needs to keep others happy, creating a dynamic that can be emotionally exhausting both for themselves and for those in relationship with them. Marcus exemplifies this pattern. He constantly texts his girlfriend throughout the day, needing reassurance that she still cares. When she doesn't respond immediately, he panics, convinced that she is going to break up with him. The anxiety that drives his behavior stems from a deep-seated belief that he is fundamentally unworthy of consistent love.

Spiritually, these individuals struggle profoundly with their relationship with God because they feel they are too imperfect and flawed to relate to a perfect God. They constantly worry about losing God's favor and may engage in excessive religious rituals seeking reassurance, yet they never feel "good enough" spiritually. Despite God's promises of unconditional love and grace, they experience persistent guilt and unworthiness. Marcus reads the Bible and prays obsessively but never feels secure in God's love, always fearing he has done something to lose God's approval. His preoccupied attachment creates a spiritual cycle of seeking and never finding the reassurance his heart desperately craves.

Fearful Attachment: The Paradox of Longing and Terror

Fearful attachment represents perhaps the most painful pattern, characterized by both a negative view of self and a negative view of others. These are individuals who possess a low sense of self-worth coupled with a deep mistrust of others. They avoid intimacy and relationships because they expect rejection or negative treatment, creating a pattern of self-protection in which they distance themselves from others to avoid being hurt. The tragic irony of this attachment style is that while they crave connection desperately, they are simultaneously too afraid to pursue it.

These individuals want relationships but expect rejection or negative treatment, often resulting in isolation or shallow interactions. Their relational pattern follows a push-pull dynamic in which they desire closeness but fear it, may sabotage relationships when they become too close, and struggle with trusting anyone. They often feel lonely but are too scared to reach out, caught in a painful cycle of unfulfilled longing.

Sophia desperately wants a close relationship with someone, but every time a potential partner shows interest, she finds reasons to push him away. Terrified of being hurt, she keeps everyone at arm's length, ensuring that her fears of rejection never have the chance to be realized—or disproven.

Spiritually, these individuals struggle intensely to build a relationship with God due to their fear of commitment and vulnerability. To build a stable relationship with God, the Heavenly Father, one must be ready to commit and to trust, precisely what fearful attachment makes nearly impossible. They want God's love but fear getting hurt, find it hard to trust God's goodness, may approach God tentatively only to pull away, and struggle with the vulnerability that authentic faith requires. Sophia longs for connection with God but feels too broken and unworthy, afraid that even God will reject her if she gets too close. Her fearful attachment creates a spiritual paralysis in which the very intimacy she craves remains perpetually out of reach.

Dismissive Attachment: The Fortress of Independence

Dismissive individuals, representing a positive view of self combined with a negative view of others, typically possess a strong sense of self-worth but hold a negative view of others. They prefer to maintain emotional distance and avoid close relationships to protect their independence and self-image, prioritizing self-reliance and often dismissing the importance of intimacy. They believe that staying detached helps preserve their autonomy and maintain emotional invulnerability.

In relationships, dismissive individuals keep people at arm's length emotionally, feel uncomfortable with too much closeness, and may seem cold or unfeeling to those who attempt to get close to them. They value independence over connection and operate with an "I don't need anyone" mentality that serves as both protection and prison. Jason has never had a serious relationship. He dates casually but never lets anyone get too close, priding himself on being independent and viewing emotional needs as weakness. What he experiences as strength, however, is actually a defensive posture born from early relational wounds.

Spiritually, dismissive individuals struggle to see the value in a relationship with God. They may view religion as unnecessary or irrelevant, keep God at a distance emotionally, and prefer to go through religious motions without heart connection. Their preference for intellectual faith over emotional intimacy creates a spirituality that is more philosophical than relational. Jason attends church occasionally but keeps God at arm's length, viewing deep faith as overly emotional or unnecessary. His dismissive attachment prevents him from experiencing the very connection that could heal the wounds that created his defensive posture in the first place.

The Formative Influence of Early Life Experiences

Research has consistently demonstrated that attachment styles are closely linked to early life experiences, particularly the relationships individuals had with their parents or caregivers. Those with secure attachment often recall positive and supportive childhood experiences and view their caregivers as important, loving figures, generally maintaining healthy perceptions of their past relationships. In contrast, individuals with preoccupied attachment may report feeling close to their parents but simultaneously express discomfort due to a lack of genuine emotional support or understanding—describing a sense of "they were there, but not really *there* for me."

Those with fearful and dismissive attachments often harbor more negative childhood memories, which may include neglect, rejection, or inconsistent caregiving. These individuals frequently report having learned early that people will hurt you, creating defensive relational strategies designed to minimize future pain. Key research findings suggest that both "goal-directed" parenting—deliberate actions like setting rules or teaching lessons—and "non-goal-directed" parenting—expressing love and emotions naturally—significantly influence a child's future attachment style. The bottom line is clear: a child's perception of their parents and the emotional quality of these early relationships play a crucial role in shaping how they interact with others as adults and, profoundly, how they relate to God.

The Critical Role of Parenting Styles

Researchers Carranza and Kilmann conducted extensive research to explore how parenting styles impact children and influence their attachment styles and relationships in adulthood. Their research focused on three key aspects of parent-child relationships: emotional relationships, parenting practices, and parental belief systems.

The emotional bond between parent and child emerged as one of the most critical factors in attachment formation, including the level of warmth, affection, and responsiveness a parent demonstrates. Parents who are attentive, nurturing, and emotionally available foster a sense of safety and security in their children, creating a foundation that supports healthy attachment and allows children to feel confident exploring the world and forming trusting relationships. Conversely, parents who are neglectful, inconsistent, or emotionally distant create uncertainty and anxiety in their children, often leading to attachment styles marked by fear of rejection, clinginess, or avoidance of intimacy. Children's early emotional experiences with parents serve as a template for future relationships, profoundly influencing how they perceive and connect with others throughout their lives—including their perception of and connection with God.

Parenting practices—the day-to-day actions, discipline methods, and strategies parents use to guide their children's behavior and development—also significantly impact attachment formation. Supportive practices such as positive reinforcement, clear communication, and consistent discipline foster self-esteem, independence, and emotional resilience, contributing to secure attachment styles that enable children to form balanced and trusting relationships. Harmful practices, including overly strict or authoritarian methods, permissiveness, or neglect, can lead to significant attachment issues. Overly controlling parenting may foster dependency or fear of autonomy, while neglectful parenting can cultivate feelings of unworthiness or distrust. The way parents approach their role as caregivers profoundly impacts their child's ability to navigate challenges, regulate emotions, and form meaningful connections.

Finally, parental belief systems—the values, attitudes, and worldviews parents hold—shape their parenting styles and the environment they create for their children. Parents who value empathy, emotional expression, and respect for individuality create nurturing environments where children feel understood and accepted. These beliefs encourage secure attachments and contribute to a positive sense of self. Conversely, parents with rigid or authoritarian worldviews may impose strict expectations or limit emotional expression, leading to feelings of inadequacy and attachment styles characterized by fear or avoidance of intimacy. Parental beliefs not only influence how children are raised but also affect how children perceive themselves and others, fundamentally shaping their expectations in future relationships and their capacity to trust in God's goodness.

Carranza and Kilmann's research confirmed that the parenting styles children experience directly shape their emotional, relational, and attachment development, with this influence extending into adulthood and affecting self-perception, relationship patterns, and conflict resolution abilities. By understanding the specific ways parenting impacts attachment, this research highlights both the importance of creating emotionally supportive and consistent environments for children and underscores the need for adults to reflect on their early experiences and, if necessary, address unresolved issues to build healthier relationships. For believers, this also reveals the critical importance of understanding how early parental relationships shape one's capacity to receive and rest in God's perfect fatherly love.

Paul Vitz's Research: Atheism and Defective Fathers

In his groundbreaking book *Faith of the Fatherless: The Psychology of Atheism*, psychologist Paul Vitz explores a provocative hypothesis regarding the relationship between people's beliefs about God and their relationships with their fathers. Drawing on biographical studies of well-known atheists including Sigmund Freud, Voltaire, and H.G. Wells, Vitz investigates how these individuals' early paternal experiences may have shaped their rejection of religious beliefs, particularly their disbelief in God. His research takes a psychological approach to atheism, suggesting that the lack of a healthy, supportive father figure can significantly influence a person's spiritual outlook.

Vitz's central claim is that many of the prominent atheists he studied experienced difficult or dysfunctional relationships with their fathers - fathers who were emotionally absent, neglectful, or otherwise "defective." These challenging paternal relationships, Vitz argues, played a pivotal role in shaping how these individuals perceived authority figures, including God. For these individuals, the idea of a loving and protective Father figure in God may have been difficult to accept given their negative experiences with their earthly fathers. The result was a rejection of God that, according to Vitz, was rooted not merely in intellectual reasoning but in deep emotional wounds.

Vitz's theory draws heavily on the psychological concept of attachment, connecting it to religious belief and suggesting that parental attachment experiences influence how people perceive and relate to God. According to Vitz, a positive, secure attachment to a father helps establish a framework for trusting relationships, while a negative paternal relationship can disrupt this attachment, making it harder to form a positive connection with a divine father figure. Children who experience emotional neglect, abandonment, or dysfunction from their fathers may struggle to trust and connect with the notion of a benevolent, omnipotent God. They might reject the idea of God as a loving and protective father figure because their early experiences with paternal authority were fraught with emotional absence, inconsistency, or harm. This, according to Vitz, may contribute to lifelong skepticism of religious beliefs, especially those centered on God as a fatherly figure.

Vitz's research challenges the notion that atheism is purely a product of intellectual reasoning or rejection of religious dogma. Instead, he argues that it is often deeply rooted in early emotional experiences and relationships, particularly those with fathers. By examining the biographies of prominent atheists, Vitz draws a compelling connection between negative paternal attachment and the rejection of God, framing atheism not merely as a philosophical or theological stance but as a psychological coping mechanism shaped by early emotional trauma.

The term "defective fathers," as used by Vitz, refers to fathers who were emotionally unavailable, neglectful, or abusive. For instance, Vitz highlights Sigmund Freud's relationship with his father, which was marked by emotional distance and a lack of warmth. Freud's father was a strict, emotionally distant figure who did not offer affection and guidance, and Freud's work, especially his theories of human development, may reflect his internal struggle with authority, including his rejection of the idea of a loving God. Similarly, the French philosopher Voltaire had a strained relationship with his father characterized by emotional neglect and lack of paternal connection, which may have contributed to Voltaire's rejection of religion, particularly his rejection of the idea of God as a loving father figure.

By comparing the biographies of these influential atheists, Vitz argues that their early paternal experiences were not mere coincidences but may have contributed to their theological and philosophical views, particularly their rejection of the concept of God as a loving, fatherly presence. His research suggests that the absence of a healthy, nurturing father figure can lead to a distorted view of God, especially in religious traditions that emphasize God as a father. This rejection of the divine father figure, according to Vitz, can extend beyond the intellectual realm, affecting emotional development and shaping relationships with others, including authority figures, throughout life.

Supporting Evidence: Links Between Parenting Styles and Attachment

Further research supports Vitz's claims about the significant role that parenting styles play in shaping attachment patterns and emotional development. Avoidant attachment is often linked to mothers who were inconsistent and fathers who were emotionally distant or cold. Children of emotionally unavailable fathers may learn to suppress their emotional needs and develop a sense of self-sufficiency and emotional detachment. These individuals often struggle with forming intimate relationships later in life and have difficulty trusting others, including God, as they have learned that emotional vulnerability leads to disappointment or abandonment.

Codependency is often associated with authoritarian fathers who are overly controlling or strict. Children raised by authoritarian fathers may grow up feeling trapped in relationships that lack emotional warmth or balance, struggling with feelings of inadequacy or fear of rejection. These attachment patterns lead to struggles in later relationships, making it challenging to form healthy, secure connections either with other people or with God.

In contrast, children raised by warm and emotionally expressive fathers tend to develop strong emotional bonds, particularly daughters. This warmth and emotional availability fosters trust and security, helping children develop positive self-worth and a healthy approach to relationships. These individuals are more likely to form secure attachments with others, including their spiritual beliefs, and to be open to experiencing the love and care associated with God as a father. Studies like those by Mallinckrodt and colleagues (1995) reveal that a father's emotional support plays a critical role in women's social development and emotional well-being. Women who have positive emotional relationships with their fathers tend to have higher self-esteem, greater social competence, and a stronger sense of emotional stability. These findings further emphasize the crucial role that paternal attachment plays in shaping overall development, including spiritual attachment and beliefs about God's character.

Victoria Secunda's Research: Father-Daughter Dynamics

Victoria Secunda has been a leading researcher in exploring father-daughter dynamics and how primary paternal figures shape a woman's relationships as an adult. Her research examined the impact of a woman's relationship with "the first man in her life" and found that a woman's attachment history with her father significantly influences the quality of her future relationships. Secunda's findings align with earlier research suggesting that individuals classified as "secure" tend to experience healthier relationships characterized by greater levels of trust, more intimacy, and better emotional connection.

Building on this foundation, Secunda identified six distinct patterns or clusters that describe the varying characteristics of fathers, providing insight into how different paternal behaviors and relationships contribute to a daughter's emotional development and attachment style. These six father archetypes offer a nuanced understanding of how fathers shape their daughters' relational templates and, consequently, their perceptions of God.

The Doting Father

The doting father is overly involved and indulgent, often granting his daughter anything she wants within certain limits, spoiling her and making her the center of his world. While this might appear benign or even loving on the surface, it creates significant distortions in how the daughter perceives relationships and God. This may lead to seeing God as a "gift-giving daddy" who exists primarily to fulfill wants and needs rather than as a sovereign Lord with purposes beyond immediate gratification.

Individuals with this perspective struggle to see themselves as part of God's greater purpose and may feel anger or disappointment when God does not meet their expectations. This view is inconsistent with the biblical understanding of God as a balanced and just Father who loves His children but also calls them to obedience, sacrifice, and participation in His redemptive purposes. Ashley's father gave her everything she wanted growing up. Now as an adult, she approaches God like a cosmic vending machine, expecting Him to give her whatever she asks for. When prayers are not answered the way she wants, she feels angry and abandoned, struggling to understand that God has purposes beyond her immediate desires and that His love is not measured by His compliance with her requests.

The Seductive Father

The seductive father exhibits inappropriate or even abusive behaviors, often sexually suggestive or self-serving in his interactions with his daughter, crossing boundaries in ways that make her uncomfortable or violate her sense of safety and dignity. This profoundly harmful pattern can result in viewing God as manipulative and self-serving, leading to deep distrust and constant questioning of God's motives. The daughter raised by a seductive father learns to ask, "What does God want from me?" rather than resting in what God has already done for her through Christ.

This distorted view creates significant barriers to a healthy spiritual relationship and makes vulnerability with God feel dangerous rather than liberating. Nicole's father made inappropriate comments about her appearance and touched her in ways that made her uncomfortable. Now she struggles to trust any authority figure, including God. She constantly questions God's motives, wondering if He is trying to manipulate or use her, making genuine faith nearly impossible. The profound violation of trust she experienced with her earthly father has created barriers to experiencing the perfect, holy love of her Heavenly Father.

The Distant Father

The distant father is physically present but emotionally absent, uninvolved or disengaged during critical attachment years. He represents the "strong, silent type" present in body but absent in heart. This pattern of paternal unavailability may lead to seeing God as detached or uninvolved, setting life into motion but remaining distant and uninvolved in personal matters. This fosters feelings of abandonment and cultivates the belief that intimacy with God is unattainable or meaningless, creating a deistic rather than relational view of the divine.

Michael's father was always working, never at his games, never interested in his life. Now he sees God the same way—existing somewhere out there but not really involved in his day-to-day struggles. Prayer feels pointless because he assumes God is not really listening or caring, mirroring the disinterest his earthly father showed. This distortion prevents him from experiencing the God who is "near to the brokenhearted" and who knows the number of hairs on his head, the God who is intimately and continuously involved in the lives of His children.

The Good Father

The good father is supportive, loving, dependable, and involved, both emotionally and physically present in his daughter's life. He balances discipline with affection, shows consistent love, and creates a secure foundation for healthy relational development. This archetype encourages a view of God as unfailing, faithful, and a source of unconditional love, leading to trust in God's care and blessings even during difficult times. This pattern aligns perfectly with the biblical understanding of God as a loving and forgiving Father who sacrificed for humanity, as expressed in Romans 5:8: "While we were yet sinners, Christ died for us."

Grace's father was present, loving, and supportive throughout her childhood. He disciplined her when needed but always with love and explanation, creating a secure attachment that translated into spiritual health. Now she has a healthy relationship with God—she trusts His goodness even in hard times, communicates openly in prayer, and rests secure in His love. Her earthly father's faithful presence created a template that allows her to receive her Heavenly Father's love without the distortions that plague those with insecure attachments.

The Demanding Father

The demanding father dominates through strict rules, constant pressure, and threats of punishment. Nothing is ever good enough, and love feels conditional on performance rather than freely given. This may lead to seeing God as a punitive figure who enforces rules with harsh consequences, always disappointed and waiting to punish mistakes. This creates a faith rooted in fear of punishment rather than love or trust, resulting in an exhausting cycle of trying to be "good enough" that can never be satisfied.

David's father had impossibly high standards and harsh punishments for any failures. Now he sees God the same way—a demanding taskmaster who is never satisfied. His faith is driven by fear rather than love, and he is constantly anxious about whether he is measuring up spiritually. This distortion prevents him from resting in the finished work of Christ and receiving the grace that God freely offers, instead trapping him in a performance-based spirituality that can never bring peace.

The Absent Father

The absent father is simply not there, either physically or emotionally, leaving a void in his daughter's life where paternal presence and guidance should be. This absence creates profound insecurity and anxiety in relationships, fostering preoccupied attachment characterized by desperate seeking for the presence and reassurance that was missing in childhood. The daughter of an absent father may struggle to believe that anyone, including God, will truly be there for her when she needs them, creating a constant anxiety about abandonment.

Correlation Between Father Archetypes and Attachment Patterns

Research by Carranza and Kilmann supports Secunda's findings, demonstrating how a father's characteristics shape a daughter's adult attachment patterns in predictable ways. The good father is linked to secure attachment and a positive, trusting view of God, resulting in healthy relationships both human and divine. The distant father is associated with dismissive attachment and a perception of God as uninvolved, creating emotional distance from both others and God. The absent father is connected to preoccupied attachment, fostering anxiety and insecurity in relationships with others and with God. The fearful attachment pattern is often tied to inconsistent or unreliable father figures, further complicating perceptions of God and creating a push-pull dynamic in all relationships.

Understanding these archetypes helps counselors and pastors address how a person's view of their earthly father influences their spiritual relationship with God. By recognizing these patterns, they can tailor therapeutic and theological approaches to guide individuals toward a healthier perception of God, rooted in the biblical view of Him as a loving, just, and faithful Father rather than the distorted view created by early relational wounds.

Detailed Characteristics and Research Findings

Secunda's research identified specific characteristics associated with each father type, providing concrete markers that help identify these patterns. The doting father is characterized by statements such as "My father always gives me anything I want," "I am closer to my father than to my mother," "My father is very protective of me," and "My father is involved in every part of my life." The seductive father is identified through profoundly troubling characteristics including "My father made comments about my body that made me feel uncomfortable," "My father touched me in ways that made me uncomfortable," and in the most severe cases, actual sexual abuse. The distant father is recognized through patterns such as "My father is the strong, silent type," "My father is not one to express their feelings," "It has always been difficult to figure out how to please my father," and "I do not feel as if I know my father very well."

The good father is identified by characteristics including "My father is strict but fair," "My father has always taken an interest in all of my activities," and "My father has always been very supportive." The absent father is characterized by "My father and I do not spend very much time together," "My father spends more time with my siblings," and "My father is more interested in my siblings." The demanding father is recognized through patterns such as "My father does not accept any deviation from their rules for any reason," "My father can be very intimidating," "My father is definitely the boss at home," and "I was afraid my father would hit me."

Carranza and Kilmann's research highlights a strong connection between women's attachment patterns and their self-perception, shaped fundamentally by their views of their fathers. Women with secure attachment tend to have a positive sense of self-worth, see themselves as valuable, trust others more easily, and form healthy relationships. Spiritually, this translates to deep trust in God as a loving Father, aligning with the "good father" archetype and creating faith rooted in trust and genuine connection rather than fear or obligation.

Those with dismissive attachment derive their sense of worth primarily within family settings and display lower interpersonal trust. Spiritually, this manifests as a "works without faith" mentality in which faith takes a backseat to deeds—a pattern observed in some religious communities where individuals go through the motions without genuine heart connection. Individuals with fearful attachment struggle with self-criticism regarding appearance, health, and worth, feeling unworthy of love, including God's love, and asking "How could God love me?" Their reluctance to engage socially extends to hesitancy in forming connections with faith communities, creating a barrier to embracing relationship with God and reflecting feelings of inadequacy and isolation.

For those with preoccupied attachment, a negative self-image dominates their worldview as they perceive themselves as inherently unworthy and often assume others share this view. Spiritually, this can lead to the belief that they are "too sinful" for God's forgiveness and a perception of God as distant or demanding, undermining trust and faith and making it profoundly difficult to accept divine love and grace despite God's repeated promises of acceptance and redemption.

The Critical Link Between Father Perception and Spiritual Formation

Carranza and Kilmann observed a clear and powerful link between perceived fatherly characteristics and adult attachment patterns. Positive father perception, exemplified by the good father, makes individuals more likely to develop secure attachment styles, creating a secure foundation that promotes trust in relationships with both others and God. Negative father perception, represented by absent, distant, or demanding fathers, makes individuals more prone to insecure attachment patterns characterized by low self-esteem, diminished trust, and a strained view of God as Father.

Their research strongly supports Paul Vitz's hypothesis that negatively perceived fatherly traits can predict insecure attachment patterns, emphasizing the critical role fathers play in shaping their daughters' self-esteem, trust, and comfort with intimacy and autonomy. Fathers who are neglectful or harsh tend to foster insecurity and negatively impact their daughters' relationships, including their spiritual connection with God. As Carranza summarized, "The results of this study suggest that parents who are supportive of and take an interest in their daughters' activities are likely to foster positive self-esteem, interpersonal trust, and comfort with intimacy and autonomy. The findings also suggest that women who do not perceive their fathers positively are more likely to report an insecure attachment pattern. Thus, a woman who perceives her father as acting in a neglectful and/or negative manner is more likely to experience lowered self-esteem and related issues of trust."

Practical Implications for Counselors and Pastors

Understanding these dynamics is absolutely essential for professionals like pastors and counselors who seek to help individuals experience spiritual healing and growth. Recognizing a client's attachment style and their early parental experiences can guide therapeutic and theological approaches to address their relational and spiritual needs in ways that honor both psychological reality and biblical truth.

Fostering a secure attachment style—which is the most conducive for forming positive relationships with God—may require helping clients reconcile with their past experiences, view God as a loving Father, and separate their earthly father's failures from God's true character. This is precisely where the gospel becomes not merely doctrinal truth but healing balm for wounded hearts. By identifying patterns of dysfunction in a client's parental history, counselors can tailor their strategies to provide emotional healing and spiritual growth, encouraging clients to turn to Christ as a source of mediation and fulfillment and helping them reframe distorted views of God.

The theological truth that must undergird all such counseling is that Jesus Christ serves as the ultimate Mediator between the wounded human heart and the perfect Heavenly Father. For those whose earthly fathers were doting, seductive, distant, absent, or demanding, Christ offers a way to know the Father as He truly is—not through the distorted lens of early relational trauma, but through the perfect revelation of God's character demonstrated in Jesus. As Jesus Himself declared, "Anyone who has seen me has seen the Father" (John 14:9). Christ both reveals the Father's true nature and repairs the breach between the wounded child and the loving God who has never failed, never abandoned, and never manipulated.

Through Christ, those with preoccupied attachment can find the security they crave, not in constant reassurance from fallible humans but in the unshakeable promise that nothing can separate them from God's love (Romans 8:38-39). Through Christ, those with fearful attachment can approach the throne of grace with confidence, knowing that they will receive mercy and find grace to help in their time of need (Hebrews 4:16). Through Christ, those with dismissive attachment can discover that genuine intimacy with God does not threaten their autonomy but establishes their true identity as beloved children of God. And through Christ, those with every manner of attachment wound can experience the healing that comes from knowing a Father who is always present, always good, always faithful, and always loving.

Moving Forward: Assessment, Understanding, and Healing

Two key takeaways from this research are particularly significant for both personal growth and pastoral care. First, assessments are valuable tools for identifying relational and personality traits. Understanding one's attachment pattern can help individuals recognize patterns in their relationships, understand their spiritual struggles, identify areas for growth and healing, and seek appropriate help. Such self-awareness is not an end in itself but rather a beginning—a diagnosis that points the way toward healing and wholeness.

Second, understanding the connection between attachment patterns and father perceptions is essential for addressing barriers to a trusting relationship with God, or "Abba Father." These insights suggest a need for further methodologies and tools to deepen our understanding, foster healthier spiritual relationships, and help people separate their earthly father's failures from God's true character. Foremost in this consideration is the link between attachment patterns, father perception, and how they reflect one's view of God as Father.

This understanding provides both sobering challenge and profound hope. The challenge is that early relational wounds run deep and shape the very templates through which individuals perceive and relate to God. These are not mere intellectual barriers that can be overcome through better arguments or clearer teaching; they are deeply embedded emotional and relational patterns that require patient, compassionate work to heal. The hope, however, is equally profound: these patterns are not permanent sentences but rather starting points for redemptive transformation. With awareness, intentional effort, therapeutic support, pastoral care, and above all God's grace, individuals can develop secure attachment and experience the fullness of relationship—both human and divine—that God designed for them.

As readers finish this chapter, they are invited to engage in honest self-reflection: Which attachment archetype best describes you? How would you characterize your father or primary father figure? How has your relationship with your father shaped your view of God? What patterns do you see in your relationships that might stem from your attachment style? What steps might you need to take to heal and develop a more secure attachment—both with people and with God?

These questions are not meant to induce guilt or despair but rather to illuminate the path toward healing. Your attachment style is not your destiny. Understanding is the first step toward healing, but understanding alone is not enough. The path forward requires courage to face painful truths, humility to seek help when needed, and faith to believe that the God who created you for relationship can also heal the relational wounds that separate you from experiencing His love fully.

The gospel declares that Christ came to heal the brokenhearted and set the captives free (Luke 4:18). For those trapped in insecure attachment patterns shaped by early relational wounds, this is not mere religious platitude but genuine good news. Through Christ, the perfect Son of the perfect Father, individuals can come to know God as He truly is—not as a projection of their earthly father's failures but as the One who has loved them with an everlasting love, the One who will never leave nor forsake them, the One in whom they can find both the security they crave and the intimacy they were created to experience.

Understanding your attachment pattern is indeed the first step toward healing. But healing itself comes through encountering the God who is not limited by your early experiences, not defined by your father's failures, and not distant despite your defenses. He is the God who pursues you with relentless love, who sent His Son to bridge every gap, and who invites you even now into the relationship your heart was made for—a relationship of perfect security, unconditional love, and unending faithfulness. That invitation stands regardless of your attachment style, your father's character, or your relational history. The question is not whether you are worthy of such love—you are not, and neither is anyone else. The question is whether you will receive it, trusting that the One who offers it is completely trustworthy, utterly faithful, and perfectly good.

CHAPTER SUMMARY: BRINGING IT ALL TOGETHER - YOUR JOURNEY FROM BROKEN TO SECURE

Congratulations on completing all twelve chapters of this book.

This achievement represents more than simply reading words on pages—it represents a willingness to engage with difficult truths about attachment theory, to explore how early relationships shape present connections, and to discover how childhood wounds affect one's relationship with God as Father. Now comes the crucial work of integration, bringing together these insights into a clear roadmap for healing. Roadmaps serve a vital dual purpose: they not only show the destination but also illuminate the path required to reach it.

The Big Picture: Synthesizing the Journey

The journey through this book has been carefully structured to build understanding progressively, moving from foundational concepts through spiritual connections to practical application. A comprehensive review of this progression reveals the integrated nature of attachment theory, spiritual formation, and healing through Christ.

Chapters 1-3: The Foundation—Understanding Attachment

The opening chapter established that attachment is far more than a mere psychology term—it represents the blueprint for all human relationships. Mary Ainsworth's Strange Situation experiment demonstrated that infants develop different attachment styles based on how their caregivers respond to them. Secure attachment emerges from consistent, loving care, while insecure avoidant attachment develops when caregivers are emotionally distant. Insecure ambivalent attachment results from inconsistent caregiving, and disorganized attachment stems from frightening or confusing caregiving experiences. The foundational truth established here is that one's earliest relationships create patterns that persist into adulthood, shaping every subsequent relationship.

The second chapter explored how these early attachment experiences continue to influence adult functioning through John Bowlby's framework of the three phases of separation: protest, despair, and detachment. These early experiences shape emotional regulation, social skills, resilience, and the fundamental ability to trust others. The concept of the "divided self" emerged as particularly significant—the internal conflict between the needing self that desires connection and the rejected self that seeks protection from pain. This chapter established the crucial truth that one's past does not remain confined to childhood but follows into every relationship throughout life.

Chapter three addressed what happens when attachment goes seriously wrong, resulting in Reactive Attachment Disorder in two distinct forms. Inhibitive RAD manifests as pushing everyone away completely, while disinhibitive RAD creates a pattern of being overly friendly with strangers while remaining unable to form deep connections. Importantly, this chapter established that even severe attachment problems can be healed through appropriate therapeutic interventions, attachment-based treatments, and supportive communities, providing hope that no attachment wound is beyond redemption.

Chapters 4-6: The Spiritual Connection—How Parents Shape One's View of God

The fourth chapter examined the influence of parental images, establishing that both mothers and fathers play unique and complementary roles in shaping attachment. Fathers often model authority, trust, and spiritual leadership, while mothers provide nurturing care and emotional regulation. Together, they create a balanced foundation for healthy relationships. This chapter revealed that attachment patterns pass through generations—but critically, that this cycle can be broken through intentional intervention and healing.

Chapter five demonstrated the interplay between attachment and spirituality, showing how attachment styles directly affect spiritual life. Secure attachment facilitates seeing God as loving and trustworthy, while insecure attachment creates a view of God as distant, punitive, or inconsistent. Avoidant attachment manifests as keeping God at arm's length emotionally. The concept of Spiritual Attachment Disorder (SAD) was introduced, along with the encouraging truth that attachment patterns can be changed through both therapeutic and spiritual practices. This chapter established the profound connection between one's relationship with an earthly father and one's capacity to relate to the Heavenly Father.

The sixth chapter explored mediators and biblical principles, examining six key family issues and their connection to biblical principles: family structure relates to one's relationship with God as Father; patterns of contact correspond to ongoing communication with God; shared values connect to time in God's Word; norms and expectations link to using Scripture as life's guide; patterns of support root in faith community; and emotional ties relate to intimacy with God. This chapter established the critical role of mediators in healing broken attachments and examined how modern culture has eroded the father's role, creating widespread attachment disruption.

Chapters 7-9: The Solution—Jesus as the Ultimate Mediator

Chapter seven introduced the concept of internal working models—the mental blueprints for relationships formed in childhood. These models can be distorted by trauma, profoundly affect how individuals see themselves, others, and God, but crucially, can be reconstructed through intentional healing. This chapter established that Christian counseling offers unique approaches combining psychological principles with theological truths to heal attachment wounds, demonstrating that internal working models are not permanent but can be reshaped through therapeutic and spiritual interventions.

The eighth chapter examined how attachment styles act as mediators between childhood trauma and adult relationship problems, with particular attention to fearful avoidant attachment—the ultimate paradox of wanting closeness while simultaneously fearing it. Most importantly, this chapter established that Jesus Christ is the ultimate Mediator who provides a safe pathway to God, offers healing through His sacrifice, and models perfect trust and security. While human mediators such as therapists and counselors provide valuable assistance, Jesus offers perfect, unchanging love that can heal the deepest wounds.

Chapter nine expanded on Jesus' unique role as Mediator, distinguishing Him from secular mediators who address only psychological and emotional dimensions. Jesus addresses the whole person—spirit, soul, and body—providing emotional healing by comforting the brokenhearted, relational reconciliation by enabling forgiveness, and spiritual renewal by restoring relationship with God. This chapter established the crucial truth that Jesus is not merely a mediator among many options but the Mediator, the only one who can fully heal attachment wounds and restore relationship with God.

Chapter 10: The Perfect Mediator—Jesus' Three Roles

This theologically rich chapter demonstrated how Jesus fulfills three roles that uniquely qualify Him as the perfect Mediator. As Prophet, He reveals God's truth perfectly, embodies God's word completely, surpasses all previous prophets, and serves as the final and complete revelation of God. As Priest, He offers the perfect sacrifice through giving Himself, provides eternal atonement rather than the temporary covering offered by animal sacrifices, intercedes for believers continually, and bridges the gap between God and humanity. As King, He reigns with perfect justice and truth, offers restoration 'to broken relationships, provides eternal security, and will return to establish His kingdom fully. These three roles—Prophet, Priest, and King—

uniquely qualify Jesus to be the perfect Mediator who can heal all attachment wounds.

Chapters 11-12: Diagnosis and Identification— Recognizing One's Patterns

Chapter eleven gave formal recognition to a struggle many face: Spiritual Attachment Disorder (SAD)—the inability to form a secure spiritual connection with God due to early attachment wounds. This disorder manifests in three ways: avoidant attachment to spirituality creates emotional detachment from God; anxious attachment to spirituality produces fear-driven faith in which one never feels "good enough"; and disorganized attachment to spirituality results in simultaneously seeking and fearing God. Most importantly, this chapter outlined concrete steps for healing: acknowledging Jesus as Lord and Savior, understanding Jesus as Mediator, considering professional help, engaging in inner healing prayer, joining a supportive faith community, and practicing journaling, intentional prayer, and mentorship. The crucial message is that Spiritual Attachment Disorder is not permanent—with intentional effort and divine grace, profound healing is available.

The final chapter provided a comprehensive framework for identifying one's attachment style through examination of four attachment types: Secure attachment reflects a positive view of self and others; Preoccupied attachment combines a negative view of self with a positive view of others; Fearful attachment represents negative views of both self and others; and Dismissive attachment pairs a positive view of self with a negative view of others. The chapter also examined six father archetypes and how they distort one's view of God: the Doting Father creates a view of God as "gift-giving daddy"; the Seductive Father produces a perception of God as manipulative; the Distant Father results in seeing God as uninvolved; the Good Father facilitates viewing God as loving and trustworthy; the Absent Father creates a sense of God as unavailable; and the Demanding Father generates a perception of God as punitive. Understanding one's attachment type and how one's father shaped one's view of God represents the essential first step toward healing.

The Central Message: Hope for Healing

If readers take away only one truth from this book, it should be this: attachment wounds are real, but they are not permanent. Several foundational truths must be embraced to begin the healing journey.

First, it is not one's fault. The attachment style developed in childhood was not a choice made by the child. Children respond to their environment in the only ways available to them, developing coping mechanisms necessary for survival. There is no shame in having developed these protective strategies, even when they now create difficulties in adult relationships.

Second, attachment wounds do affect one's life in profound and pervasive ways. Early attachment experiences shape how individuals relate to others, see themselves, handle conflict, experience intimacy, and relate to God. Denying this reality will not make it disappear. Acknowledging these effects represents the essential first step toward healing. Without honest recognition of how attachment wounds influence present functioning, meaningful change remains impossible.

Third, and most importantly, change is possible. Attachment patterns can be reshaped through therapeutic interventions including professional counseling, spiritual interventions such as prayer, Scripture engagement, and faith community participation, and ultimately through relationship with the ultimate Mediator, Jesus Christ. Individuals can develop secure attachment regardless of where they began, regardless of how severe their early wounds, and regardless of how long they have lived with insecure attachment patterns.

Fourth, God is not like one's earthly father. If an earthly father failed to provide secure attachment, this crucial truth must be embraced: God is fundamentally different from any human parent. An absent father may have created expectations of abandonment, but God promises, "I will never leave you nor forsake you" (Hebrews 13:5). A harsh father may have instilled fear, but God says, "Come to me, all who are weary and burdened, and I will give you rest" (Matthew 11:28). An unreliable father may have destroyed trust, but God declares, "Jesus Christ is the same yesterday and today and forever" (Hebrews 13:8). A father whose love felt conditional may have created performance anxiety, but God affirms, "Nothing can separate us from the love of God" (Romans 8:38-39). These are not merely comforting religious platitudes but ontological realities about God's unchanging character.

Fifth, Jesus bridges the gap between human brokenness and divine wholeness. No one must fix themselves before approaching God—this is precisely what Jesus accomplishes as Mediator. He takes human brokenness and offers His wholeness, bridging the seemingly unbridgeable gap between attachment wounds and God's healing, making relationship with God possible for even the most wounded individual.

A Roadmap for Healing

Understanding the problem represents only the beginning. What follows is a comprehensive, step-by-step roadmap for healing attachment wounds and developing secure attachment with God and others.

Step One: Identify Your Attachment Style

Healing begins with honest self-assessment. Readers must examine Chapter 12 and honestly evaluate which attachment type best describes their relational patterns, which father archetype characterizes their father or primary father figure, and how this has shaped their view of God. Honesty is non-negotiable at this stage—one cannot heal what one refuses to acknowledge. The temptation to minimize wounds, excuse parental failures, or present oneself in a more favorable light must be resisted. Authentic healing requires authentic assessment.

Step Two: Understand Your Internal Working Models

The next step involves reflection on the mental blueprints developed in childhood. These internal working models answer crucial questions: What do I believe about myself—am I worthy of love? What do I believe about others—can people be trusted? What do I believe about God—is He loving or punitive? These beliefs, often operating unconsciously, drive relational patterns and must be brought into conscious awareness. Writing these beliefs on paper serves a therapeutic function, making them less powerful through the act of externalizing what has remained internal and unexamined.

Step Three: Challenge Distorted Beliefs

Having identified internal working models, the work of challenging and replacing them begins. Each distorted belief must be examined: Where did this belief originate—usually from early experiences? Is it true - often it is not? What does Scripture say instead - God's truth versus internalized lies? The process of replacing lies with truth becomes central to healing. The lie "I am unlovable" must be confronted with the truth "God loved me while I was still a sinner" (Romans 5:8). The belief "I cannot trust anyone" must be challenged with "God is faithful; he will not let you be tempted beyond what you can bear" (1 Corinthians 10:13). The conviction "I am too broken for God" must be replaced with "He heals the brokenhearted and binds up their wounds" (Psalm 147:3). This is not mere positive thinking but the renewal of the mind through engagement with God's revealed truth.

Step Four: Seek Professional Help

The healing journey should not be attempted in isolation. Professional assistance provides essential support and expertise that accelerates healing and prevents common pitfalls. Individuals should seek a therapist trained in attachment theory, especially one who specializes in trauma, and preferably a Christian counselor who integrates faith and psychology. Additionally, a pastor or spiritual mentor—someone mature in faith who understands attachment wounds and can walk alongside someone through spiritual healing—provides crucial spiritual guidance. Support groups with others on the same healing journey offer accountability and encouragement, creating a community of shared experience and mutual support.

The cultural stigma around seeking professional help must be confronted and rejected. Seeking help is not a sign of weakness but rather evidence of strength, wisdom, and commitment to healing. The false belief that one should be able to heal alone often represents another manifestation of insecure attachment, reflecting either the dismissive attachment's false self-sufficiency or the fearful attachment's reluctance to trust others. True healing almost always requires the assistance of others.

Step Five: Engage in Spiritual Practices

Alongside professional help, engagement in practices that foster spiritual healing accelerates the healing process. Journaling provides a means to reflect on Scripture daily, process emotions through writing, track spiritual growth, and record prayers and God's responses. The practice of writing thoughts and feelings externalizes internal struggles, making them more manageable and creating a record of God's faithfulness over time.

Intentional prayer differs from rote or casual prayer. It includes contemplative prayer—sitting in silence with God, waiting in

His presence without agenda; praying Scripture back to God, allowing His own words to shape prayer; practicing listening prayer, which involves waiting for God to speak rather than merely presenting requests; and maintaining honesty about struggles, fears, and doubts rather than presenting a sanitized version of oneself to God.

Inner healing prayer specifically addresses attachment wounds by inviting God into painful memories, asking Jesus to reveal His presence in those moments of wounding, allowing the Holy Spirit to bring truth and healing to distorted perceptions, and replacing lies absorbed in childhood with God's truth. This practice recognizes that Jesus exists outside of time and can minister to the wounded child within, bringing healing to memories that continue to exert influence in the present.

Scripture meditation focuses particularly on passages about God's character, especially those that contradict false beliefs formed through early attachment wounds. This practice allows God's Word to renew the mind, as Paul commands in Romans 12:2, gradually transforming distorted mental models through sustained engagement with truth.

Step Six: Join a Faith Community

Healing cannot occur in isolation—connection with a faith community is essential. Individuals need a local church that emphasizes grace over law, a small group where vulnerability is safe, mentorship from spiritually mature believers who can provide guidance and encouragement, and opportunities to serve others, recognizing that healing is often solidified through helping others heal.

When seeking a faith community, individuals should look for one that accepts imperfect people without judgment, emphasizes God's love over rigid rules, provides safe spaces for honesty about struggles and doubts, and models healthy relationships through authentic connection rather than superficial niceness. A healthy faith community becomes a corrective emotional experience, providing the secure attachment that was missing in childhood and creating new relational templates that can be generalized to other relationships, including relationship with God.

Step Seven: Embrace Jesus as Your Mediator

This represents the most crucial step in the healing journey. Intellectual understanding that Jesus is the Mediator, while necessary, is insufficient—this truth must be experienced relationally and emotionally, not merely assented to cognitively.

Daily surrender creates a rhythm of consciously giving attachment wounds to Jesus each morning, explicitly naming specific struggles: "Jesus, I bring you my fear of abandonment, my difficulty trusting, my shame, my spiritual distance. Be my Mediator today. Bridge the gap between my brokenness and God's wholeness." This practice acknowledges ongoing need for His mediating work while also expressing faith that He is actively engaged in providing it.

Experiencing His presence moves beyond merely reading about Jesus to spending time with Him through prayer that includes both talking and listening, through Scripture reading that allows Him to speak personally, through worship that expresses one's heart to Him, and through community that manifests His presence through His people. Jesus is not a concept to be understood but a person to be known.

Receiving His love may be the most difficult aspect of this step, particularly for those with insecure attachment. Practical exercises help develop capacity to receive sitting quietly and imagining Jesus embracing the wounded child within; reading passages about God's love and allowing them to penetrate emotional defenses; when shame arises, remembering that Jesus died for sinners while they were still sinners; and learning to let Him love without first earning that love through performance. For those with preoccupied attachment who constantly seek reassurance, this means learning to rest in His unchanging love rather than constantly seeking new evidence of it. For those with dismissive attachment who keep others at a distance, this means allowing vulnerability and emotional connection. For those with fearful attachments who want love but fear it, this means taking small steps toward trust despite fear.

Trusting the process requires understanding that Jesus' mediation is not instant transformation but a journey. Individuals must trust that He is working even when they do not feel it, that healing takes time and cannot be rushed, that setbacks are normal aspects of the healing process rather than indicators of failure, and that He remains patient with each person's unique pace of healing.

Step Eight: Be Patient with Yourself

Healing from attachment wounds is a marathon, not a sprint. Patterns developed over years will not change overnight. There will be good days and difficult days. Progress is rarely linear—there will be advances and retreats, growth and regression. Setbacks do not mean failure but rather represent the normal rhythm of deep psychological and spiritual healing. God exercises patience with His children, and individuals must learn to extend that same patience to themselves.

Celebrating small victories becomes important: the first time one prays with genuine vulnerability; when one takes the risk of sharing one's story with a trusted person; the moment one successfully challenges a false belief with truth; any step, however small, toward secure attachment. These small victories, accumulated over time, represent genuine progress even when the final goal seems distant.

Step Nine: Break the Cycle

For those who have children or plan to have them, one of the most powerful motivations for healing is breaking the cycle of insecure attachment. When individuals heal their own attachment wounds, they stop passing them to the next generation, model healthy relationships for their children, give them the secure attachment they themselves did not have, and create a legacy of healing instead of pain. This work serves not only personal healing but also generational transformation.

Even for those without children, breaking the cycle matters. The influence individuals have on nieces, nephews, friends' children, or children in their faith community means that their healing ripples outward, creating increasingly wide circles of impact. Healed people create healthier communities, which in turn produce more securely attached individuals.

Step Ten: Help Others

Once healing has been experienced, or even while still in process, helping others solidifies one's own healing and gives meaning to past pain. Sharing one's story when appropriate, encouraging others on the healing journey, being a safe person for someone else to trust, and mentoring someone struggling with attachment wounds transforms personal suffering into redemptive purpose. Pain that seemed meaningless when experienced becomes pregnant with meaning when used to help others avoid or heal from similar wounds.

Common Obstacles and How to Overcome Them

As individuals embark on this healing journey, they will inevitably face obstacles. Anticipating these challenges and developing strategies to overcome them increases the likelihood of persevering to healing.

The first common obstacle is the belief that looking at one's past is too painful. This is true—it is painful. But avoiding this pain keeps individuals stuck in patterns that continue to cause pain in different ways. The solution involves going at one's own pace without rushing, working with a professional who can help process memories safely, remembering that the pain of staying stuck ultimately exceeds the pain of healing, and trusting that Jesus is present in the pain, not asking individuals to face it alone.

The second obstacle is the claim that one does not have time for healing work. The truth is that individuals do not have time not to engage in healing. Attachment wounds affect every area of life, creating inefficiencies, conflicts, and missed opportunities that consume far more time than would be devoted to healing. The solution includes starting small with achievable commitments such as ten minutes of journaling daily, making healing a priority by scheduling it like any important appointment, realizing that emotional and spiritual health matters as much as physical health, and remembering that healing now saves both time and pain later.

The third obstacle is the fear that one cannot change. This fear, while understandable given past experiences and present struggles, contradicts both research and biblical promises. The solution involves remembering that research consistently demonstrates attachment styles are malleable, trusting in God's power to transform according to His promises, taking one small step at a time rather than being overwhelmed by the magnitude of needed change, and finding a support system that believes in one's capacity for transformation even when one's own faith wavers.

The fourth obstacle is the belief that one's faith is not strong enough for healing. Jesus does not require perfect faith but merely willingness. The solution includes remembering the father who cried out to Jesus, "I believe; help my unbelief!" (Mark 9:24)—Jesus honored this imperfect faith and can honor similarly imperfect faith today. Bringing doubts to Jesus rather than hiding them acknowledges His capacity to handle honest struggle. Allowing others to carry faith when one's own feels weak reflects the biblical principle of bearing one another's burdens. Trusting that even mustard-seed faith suffices, as Jesus Himself taught (Matthew 17:20), frees individuals from the paralyzing belief that they must attain some threshold of faith before beginning.

The fifth obstacle is the discouragement that comes from previous failed attempts at healing. These previous attempts were not failures but learning experiences that provide wisdom for the current attempt. The solution involves using the comprehensive approach outlined in this book rather than isolated strategies, getting professional help rather than attempting to heal alone, addressing both psychological and spiritual dimensions simultaneously rather than treating them as separate issues, and remembering that Jesus specializes in second chances—and third, and fourth, and as many as are needed.

The sixth obstacle is the practical concern that one cannot afford therapy. While financial constraints are real, there are options even with limited resources. Solutions include looking for sliding-scale counseling centers that adjust fees based on income, asking one's church if they maintain a counseling fund to help members access mental health services, checking whether insurance covers mental health services at a higher rate than assumed, considering online therapy options that are often more affordable than in-person sessions, joining free support groups that provide community and practical help, and utilizing the free spiritual practices outlined in this book that cost nothing but time and commitment.

The Ultimate Truth: No One Is Beyond Healing

No matter how severe one's attachment wounds, no matter how dysfunctional one's childhood, no matter how many times one has tried and seemingly failed, no matter how distant God feels, no matter how broken one's relationships—no one is beyond healing. This is not wishful thinking or religious optimism, but truth rooted in the character and power of God.

The same Jesus who healed the paralytic, restored the demon-possessed man, forgave the woman caught in adultery, welcomed the prodigal son home, and rose from the dead - that same Jesus stand ready to heal our attachment wounds. He specializes in the impossible. He transforms the broken. He restores what has been lost. He bridges gaps that seem unbridgeable. His power is not limited by the severity of wounds, the length of time they have remained unhealed, or the number of previous failed attempts at healing.

Final Encouragement

As readers close this book and begin their healing journey, several crucial truths must be remembered and returned to whenever discouragement threatens to derail progress.

First, each person is deeply loved by God - not because of what they do, what they have accomplished, or how well they have healed, but because of who they are: His children, created in His image, objects of His eternal affection.

Second, attachment wounds do not define anyone - they are part of one's story but not the conclusion of it. God is writing a new chapter, one of redemption and restoration, and that story is not finished.

Third, Jesus has already accomplished the hardest work - He has bridged the gap between human brokenness and God's wholeness through His death and resurrection. The healing offered is not something individuals must achieve through their own efforts but something they receive through His finished work at the cross.

Fourth, healing is available - not merely as a theoretical possibility but as a practical reality through the steps outlined in this book, through the power of the Holy Spirit, and through the faithful presence of Christ as our faithful Mediator.

Fifth, no one is alone in this journey - God walks with His children, the Holy Spirit guides them, Jesus intercedes for them, and a community of believers surrounds them. The isolation that characterizes early attachment wounds need not characterize the healing process.

Sixth, pain is not of the Lord but it has purpose in God's economy. He will use individual healing to help others, breaking cycles and bringing hope to those who suffer from similar wounds. Pain that seemed meaningless becomes redemptive when offered to God for His purposes.

Seventh, the journey is worth every difficult step - the freedom, peace, and intimacy on the other side of healing exceeds what can be imagined from the wounded side. Those who have completed this journey testify unanimously that they would go through it again for the transformation experienced.

An Invitation

This book has provided knowledge and understanding. Now comes the time for action. God is extending an invitation to step out of the shadows of the past, experience the healing longed for, develop secure attachments with Him and others, break the cycles that have held families captive for generations, and live in the freedom and wholeness He designed for human flourishing from creation.

The invitation stands open. The path has been illuminated. The Mediator is ready and waiting. The question that remains is whether readers will accept this invitation and take the first step today. Healing does not happen through passive reading or intellectual understanding alone but through active engagement with the healing process, courageous vulnerability, and persistent faith that God is faithful to complete what He has begun.

A Blessing for the Journey

May readers experience the healing they seek. May they know, deep in their souls, that they are loved unconditionally by their Heavenly Father. May Jesus, the perfect Mediator, bridge every gap between their wounds and God's wholeness. May the Holy Spirit guide, comfort, and transform them from the inside out. May they develop secure attachment - with God, with others, and with themselves. May they break the cycles of pain in their family lines and create legacies of healing. May they experience the freedom, peace, and intimacy that God designed for humanity from the beginning. And may they, in turn, become healing presences in the lives of others, extending the grace they have received.

Your healing journey can begin right here! Right now! Take the first step. Our Father in Heaven awaits with outstretched arms, ready to receive every wounded child (no matter the age) and begin the work of restoration that only He can accomplish. The invitation has been extended.

Will you declare Jesus as both your Lord and Savior?

The path has been marked.

The Mediator stands ready.

Will you take His hand?

If you have been moved by what you experienced here, then reach out to us: info@oceanbiblicalcounseling.com and let us know!

References

i. Ainsworth, M. D., Blehar, M.C., Waters, E., & Wall, S. (1978). Patterns of Ainsworth, M. D. S., Blehar, M. C., Waters, E., & Wall, S. (1978). Attachment: A psychological study of the strange situation. Lawrence Erlbaum Associates.

ii. American Psychiatric Association. (1994). Diagnostic and statistical manual of mental disorders (4th ed., Text Rev.). Washington, DC: Author.

iii. Argles, P. (1984). The threat of separation in family conflict. The Journal of Contemporary Social Work, 62(6), 610–614.

iv. Baron, R. M., & Kenny, D. A. (1986). The moderator-mediator variable distinction in social psychological research: Conceptual, strategic, and statistical considerations. Journal of Personality and Social Psychology, 51(6), 1173–1182.

v. Bartholomew, K., & Horowitz, L. M. (1991). Attachment styles among young adults: A test of a four-category model. Journal of Personality and Social Psychology, 61(2), 226–244.

vi. Baucom, D. H. (1987). Attributions in distressed relations: How can we explain them? In S. Duck & D. Perlman (Eds.), Heterosexual relations, marriage, and divorce (pp. 177–206). Sage.

vii.   Bingle, R. G., & Bagley, G. J. (1992). Self-esteem and perceived quality of romantic and family relationships in young adults. Journal of Research in Personality, 26(4), 340–356.

viii.   Bowlby, J. (1958). The nature of the child's tie to his mother. International Journal of Psychoanalysis, 39, 350–373.

ix.   Bowlby, J. (1969). Attachment and loss: Vol. 1. Attachment. Basic Books.

x.   Bowlby, J. (1973). Attachment and loss: Vol. 2. Separation. Penguin.

xi.   Bowlby, J. (1979). Attachment and loss: Vol. 3. Loss, sadness, and depression. Basic Books.

xii.   Bowlby, J. (1982). Attachment and loss: Retrospect and prospect. American Journal of Orthopsychiatry, 52(4), 664–678.

xiii.   Bowlby, J. (1988). A secure base: Parent-child attachment and healthy human development. Basic Books.

xiv.   Bradbury, T. N., Beach, S. R. H., Fincham, F. D., & Nelson, G. M. (1996). Attributions and behavior in functional and dysfunctional marriages. Journal of Consulting and Clinical Psychology, 64(3), 569–576.

xv. Bradbury, T. N., & Fincham, F. D. (1990). Attributions in marriage: Review and critique. Psychological Bulletin, 107(1), 3–33.

xvi. Carranza, L. V., & Kilmann, P. R. (2000). Links between perceived parent characteristics and attachment variables for young women from intact families. Adolescence, 35(138), 295–312.

xvii. Collins, N. L., & Read, S. J. (1990). Adult attachment, working models, and relationship quality in dating couples. Journal of Personality and Social Psychology, 58(4), 644–663.

xviii. Dickie, J. R., Aiega, L. V., Kobyiak, J. R., & Nixon, K. M. (2006). Mother, father, and self: Sources of young adults' God concepts. Journal of the Scientific Study of Religion, 45(1), 57–68.

xix. Dodge, K. A., Bates, J. E., & Pettit, G. S. (1990). Mechanisms in the cycle of violence. Science, 250(4988), 1678–1683.

xx. Dodge, K. A., Pettit, G. S., Bates, J. E., & Valente, E. (1995). Social-information-processing patterns mediate the effect of early physical abuse on later conduct problems. Journal of Abnormal Psychology, 104(4), 632–643.

xxi. Erikson, E. H. (1963). Childhood and society (2nd ed.). W. W. Norton.

xxii.   Feeney, J., & Noller, P. (1990). Attachment style as a predictor of adult romantic relationships. Journal of Personality and Social Psychology, 58(2), 281–291.

xxiii. Fisher, J. L., & Crawford, D. W. (1992). Codependency and parenting styles. Journal of Adolescent Research, 7(3), 352–363.

xxiv.   Fonagy, P., Steele, M., Steele, H., Leigh, T., Kennedy, R., Mattoon, G., Target, M., & Gerber, A. (1996). The relation of attachment status, psychiatric classification, and response to psychotherapy. Journal of Consulting and Clinical Psychology, 64(1), 22–31.

xxv.   Gove, W. R., & Crutchfield, R. D. (1982). The family and juvenile delinquency. In J. Q. Wilson (Ed.), Crime and public policy (pp. 217–250). ICS Press.

xxvi.   Hagestad, G. O. (1987). Parent-child relations in later life: Trends and gaps in past research. In J. Lancaster, J. Altmann, A. S. Rossi, & L. Sherrod (Eds.), Parenting across the life span: Biosocial dimensions (pp. 405–427). Aldine de Gruyter.

xxvii. Hazan, C., & Shaver, P. (1987). Romantic love conceptualized as an attachment process. Journal of Personality and Social Psychology, 52(3), 511–524.

xxviii. Latty-Mann, H. (1989). The influence of family of origin dynamics on the etiology of adult attachment styles and love styles: With a special focus on adult children of alcoholics (Unpublished master's thesis). University of South Carolina, Columbia, SC.

xxix. Latty-Mann, H. (1991). An intergenerational approach to studying the influence of family of origin dynamics on the etiology of adult attachment styles: With a special focus on adult children of alcoholics (Unpublished doctoral dissertation). University of South Carolina, Columbia, SC.

xxx. Levinson, D. J. (1978). The seasons of a man's life. New York: Knopf.

xxxi. Main, M., & Solomon, J. (1986). Discovery of an insecure-disorganized/disoriented attachment pattern: Procedures, findings, and implications for the classification of behavior. In T. Berry Brazelton (Ed.), Affective development in infancy (pp. 95–124). Norwood, NJ: Ablex.

xxxii. Main, M., Kaplan, N., & Cassidy, J. (1985). Security in infancy, childhood, and adulthood: A move to the level of representation. In I. Bretherton & E. Waters (Eds.), Growing points of attachment theory and research. Monographs of the Society for Research in Child Development, 66–104.

xxxiii. Mallinckrodt, B., Coble, H. M., & Gantt, D. L. (1995). Attachment patterns in the psychotherapy relationship:

Development of client attachment to therapist scale. Journal of Consulting Psychology, 42, 307–317.

xxxiv. McCarthy, G., & Taylor, A. (1999). Avoidant/ambivalent attachment style as a mediator between abusive childhood experiences and adult relationship difficulties. Journal of Child Psychology and Psychiatry, 40(3), 465–477.

xxxv. New American Standard Bible. (1995). New American Standard Bible (NASB). Lockman Foundation.

xxxvi. Nicolosi, J. (1991). Reparative therapy of male homosexuality: A new clinical approach. Oxford, UK: Rowman & Littlefield Publishers.

xxxvii. Nicolosi, J. (2016). Shame and attachment loss: The practical work of reparative therapy. Liberal Mind Publishing.

xxxviii. Page, T. (1999). The attachment partnership as a conceptual base for exploring the impact of child maltreatment. Child and Adolescent Social Work Journal, 16(5), 419–437.

xxxix. Rosenstein, D. S., & Horowitz, H. A. (1996). Adolescent attachment and psychopathology. Journal of Consulting and Clinical Psychology, 64(2), 244–253.

xl. Rotter, J. B. (1967). A new scale for the measurement of interpersonal trust. A paper summarizing an investigation supported by a grant from the National Institute of Mental Health.

xli. Schneider, B. H., Atkinson, L., & Tardif, C. (2001). Child-parent attachment and children's peer relations: A quantitative review. Developmental Psychology, 37(1), 86–100.

xlii. Secunda, V. (1992). Women and their fathers: The sexual and romantic impact of the first man in your life. New York: Delacorte Press.

xliii. Strobel, L. (2000). The case for faith: A journalist investigates the toughest objections to Christianity. Grand Rapids, MI: Zondervan.

xliv. Styron, T., & Janoff-Bulman, R. (1997). Childhood attachment and abuse: Long-term effects on adult attachment, depression, and conflict resolution. Child Abuse & Neglect, 21(10), 1015–1023.

xlv. Thompson, A. E., & Kaplan, C. A. (1999). Emotionally abused children presenting to child psychiatry clinics. Child Abuse & Neglect, 23(2), 191–196.

xlvi. Vitz, P. C. (1958). The psychology of atheism. Truth: An International Interdisciplinary Journal of Christian Thought, 28.

xlvii. Vitz, P. C. (1999). Faith of the fatherless: The psychology of atheism. Dallas, TX: Spence Publishing.

xlviii. Weiss, B., Dodge, K. A., Bates, J. E., & Pettit, G. S. (1992). Some consequences of early harsh discipline: Child aggression and maladaptive social information processing style. Child Development, 63(6), 1321–1335.

xlix. Wilson, S. L. (2001). Attachment disorders: Review and current status. The Journal of Psychology, 135(1), 37–51.

l. Zeanah, C. H. (1996). Beyond insecurity: A reconceptualization of attachment disorders in infancy. Journal of Consulting and Clinical Psychology, 64(1), 42–52.